CONCEPTIS PUZZLES

COLOSSAL KAKURO

72 MASSIVELY MIND-BENDING PUZZLES

PUZZLE
WRIGHT
PRESS

New York

PUZZLE WRIGHT PRESS

New York

An Imprint of Sterling Publishing Co., Inc.

ISBN 978-1-4549-3539-1

For information about custom editions, special sales, and premium purchases,
please contact specialsales@unionsquareandco.com.

Manufactured in Malaysia

2   4   6   8   10   9   7   5   3   1

unionsquareandco.com

Cover design by Victor Mingovits

CONTENTS

INTRODUCTION

Kakuro puzzles are half sudoku, half crossword, and use a combination of logic and basic arithmetic. The rules are very simple:

Fill all the empty squares using the numbers 1 to 9 so that the sum of each horizontal set of digits equals the number in the black triangle to its left, and the sum of each vertical set of digits equals the number in the black triangle above it. No number may be used in the same sum more than once. (A number can be repeated in the same row or column if the numbers are separated by a black square.)

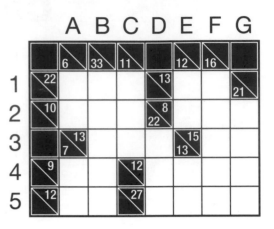

Let's try solving the sample kakuro puzzle at right to see how it works.

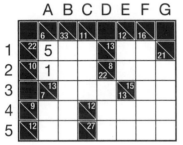

Step 1

Look at the sum of 22 in row 1. There are only two ways that three digits can total 22 without repeating a digit: $5 + 8 + 9$ and $6 + 7 + 9$. However, square A1 must be smaller than 6 because of the sum that adds up to 6 in column A. Therefore the only number possible in A1 is 5 (and 1 can be placed in A2 to complete that sum).

Step 2

From step 1 we know that B1 and C1 must contain 8 and 9, though we don't yet know in which order. Let's look at the sum that adds up to 11 in column C. If the 9 is in square C1, then C2 and C3 must both contain 1, which is not allowed. This means that C1 must be 8 and B1 must be 9.

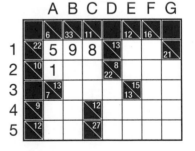

Step 3

In column C, we are now left with two empty squares that must add up to 3. The only combination of numbers for that sum is $1 + 2$, but, again, we don't know what order they go in. However, square A2 already contains 1, so the number in C2 must be 2. Completing column C and row 2 is now straightforward.

Step 4

Let's look at the sum of 16 in column F. This is called a "unique sum" because there is only one five-number combination that adds up to 16: $1 + 2 + 3 + 4 + 6$. (A list of all unique sums appears on the bottom of the next page for easy reference.) Since the sum is unique, we know all the numbers in it, but we don't know in which order they appear. Now let's examine the sum of 15 in row 3. There are only two combinations possible: $6 + 9$ and $7 + 8$. Since square F3 is the crossing point, it must contain 6, which is the only common number for both sums. This leads to placing a 9 in G3.

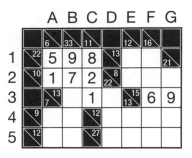

Step 5

For the sum of 13 in row 1, the only possible combinations are $4 + 9$, $5 + 8$, and $6 + 7$. However, this sum crosses the partially filled-in sum in column F, which is still missing 1, 2, 3, and 4. The only common number for F1 is 4. We can now place 9 in E1 and 3 in E2.

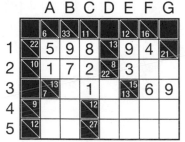

Step 6

The sum of 8 in row 2 still has two empty squares that add up to 5. There are two possible combinations: $1 + 4$ and $2 + 3$. The $2 + 3$ combination is not allowed because this sum already contains 3, and square F2 can't have a 4 in it because the vertical sum in that column already contains 4. This means that F2 must be 1 and G2 must be 4.

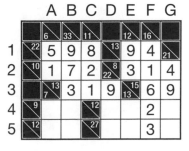

Step 7

The sum in column F is now missing only 2 and 3. Let's take a close look at the sum of 27 in row 5. If square F5 contained 2, then the remaining three squares would add up to 25. But this is not possible, because the largest possible sum of three digits is $7 + 8 + 9 = 24$. Therefore F5 is 3 and F4 is 2.

Step 8

We can now use a special solving technique in the right-hand side of the puzzle. If we add up the totals of all the sums in columns D, E, F, and G we get $22 + 12 + 13 + 16 + 21 = 84$. When we add up the horizontal sums in the same area, excluding square D3, we get $13 + 8 + 15 + 12 + 27 = 75$. This means that D3 is responsible for the difference between the vertical and horizontal totals, and therefore that square must be $84 - 75 = 9$. Now a 3 can be placed in B3 to complete the sum of 13 in that row.

Step 9

Let's go back to the sum of 27 in row 5, which has three empty squares that add up to 24. These three empty squares now form their own unique sum; the only possible combination is $7+8+9$, in some order. However, the 9 can't be in D5 or G5 because both of the vertical sums crossing those squares already contain the digit 9, so the only place left for the 9 is E5. We can now also place 4 in E4 by simple calculation.

Step 10

The sum of 12 in row 4 has two empty squares that add up to 6. The possible combinations are $2+4$ and $1+5$, but obviously only the $1+5$ is legal. We now need to determine which square is 1 and which is 5. If we place 1 in D4, then D5 would have to be larger than 9. Therefore D4 must be 5 and G4 must be 1, and we can now complete columns D and G with 8 in D5 and 7 in G5.

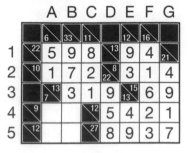

Step 11

Finally, let's examine the sum of 33 in column B. There are two empty squares that add up to 14; the only possible combinations are $5+9$ and $6+8$. But 9 is already used in column B, so we're left with $6+8$. If we choose 6 for square B5, then A5 would also have to be 6; therefore 8 is the digit in B5. Completing the remaining squares B4, A4, and A5 is now straightforward.

In this book you'll find 72 extra-large kakuro puzzles; the first 12 (pages 7–18) are hard, the next 30 (pages 19–48) are very hard, and the last 30 (pages 49–78) are very *very* hard. Enjoy!

UNIQUE SUMS					
Sum	Squares	Combination	Sum	Squares	Combination
3	2	1+2	22	6	1+2+3+4+5+7
4	2	1+3	38	6	3+5+6+7+8+9
16	2	7+9	39	6	4+5+6+7+8+9
17	2	8+9	28	7	1+2+3+4+5+6+7
6	3	1+2+3	29	7	1+2+3+4+5+6+8
7	3	1+2+4	41	7	2+4+5+6+7+8+9
23	3	6+8+9	42	7	3+4+5+6+7+8+9
24	3	7+8+9	36	8	1+2+3+4+5+6+7+8
10	4	1+2+3+4	37	8	1+2+3+4+5+6+7+9
11	4	1+2+3+5	38	8	1+2+3+4+5+6+8+9
29	4	5+7+8+9	39	8	1+2+3+4+5+7+8+9
30	4	6+7+8+9	40	8	1+2+3+4+6+7+8+9
15	5	1+2+3+4+5	41	8	1+2+3+5+6+7+8+9
16	5	1+2+3+4+6	42	8	1+2+4+5+6+7+8+9
34	5	4+6+7+8+9	43	8	1+3+4+5+6+7+8+9
35	5	5+6+7+8+9	44	8	2+3+4+5+6+7+8+9
21	6	1+2+3+4+5+6	45	9	1+2+3+4+5+6+7+8+9

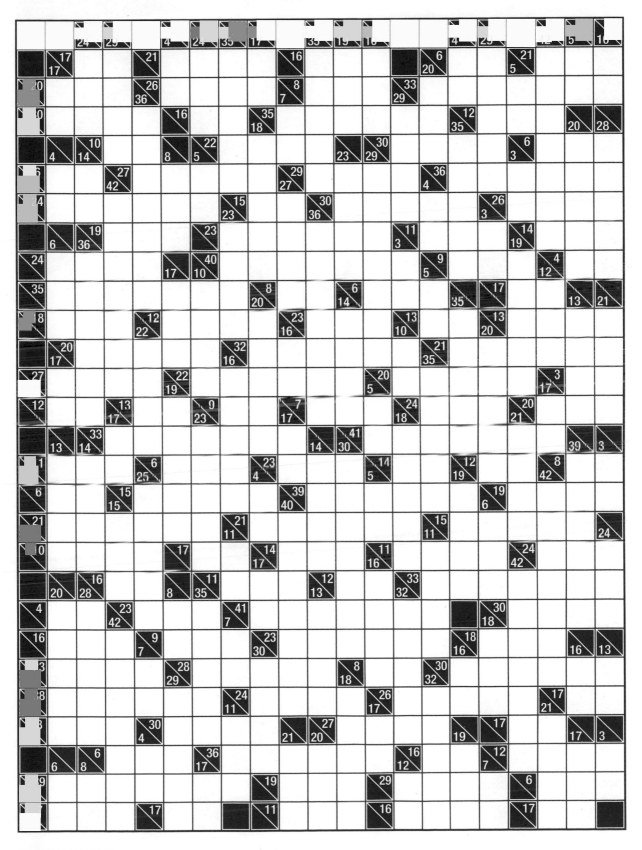

ANSWER, PAGE 79

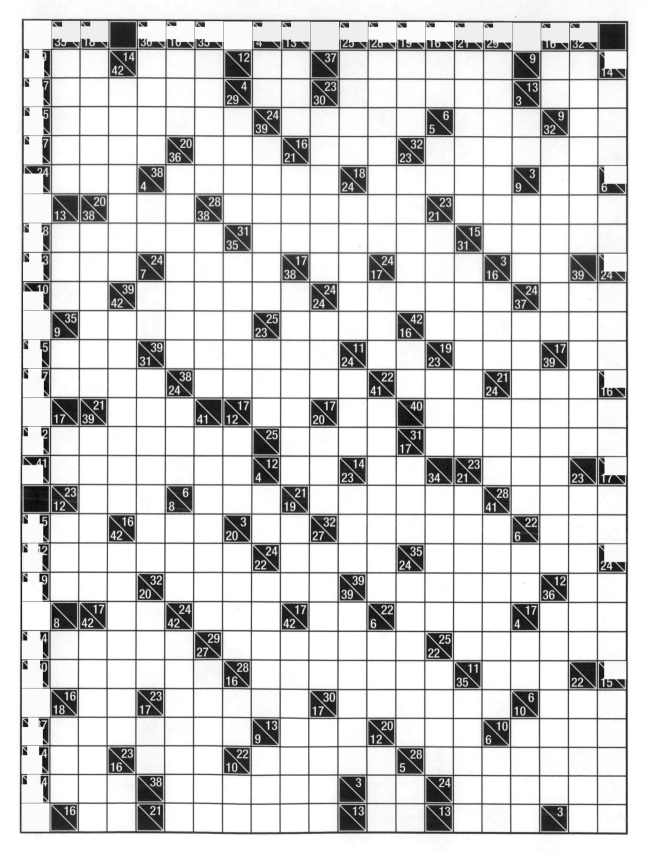

ANSWER, PAGE 79

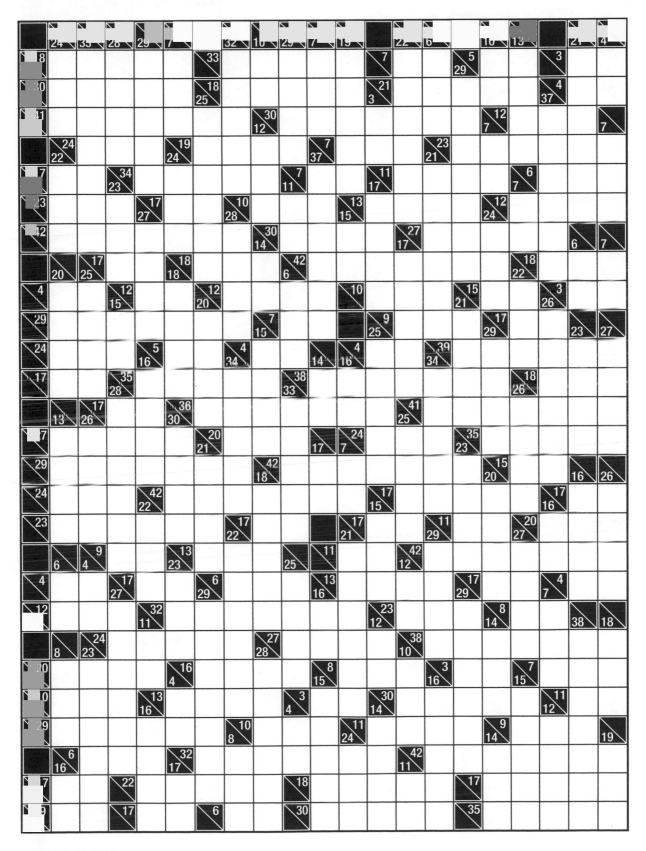

ANSWER, PAGE 79

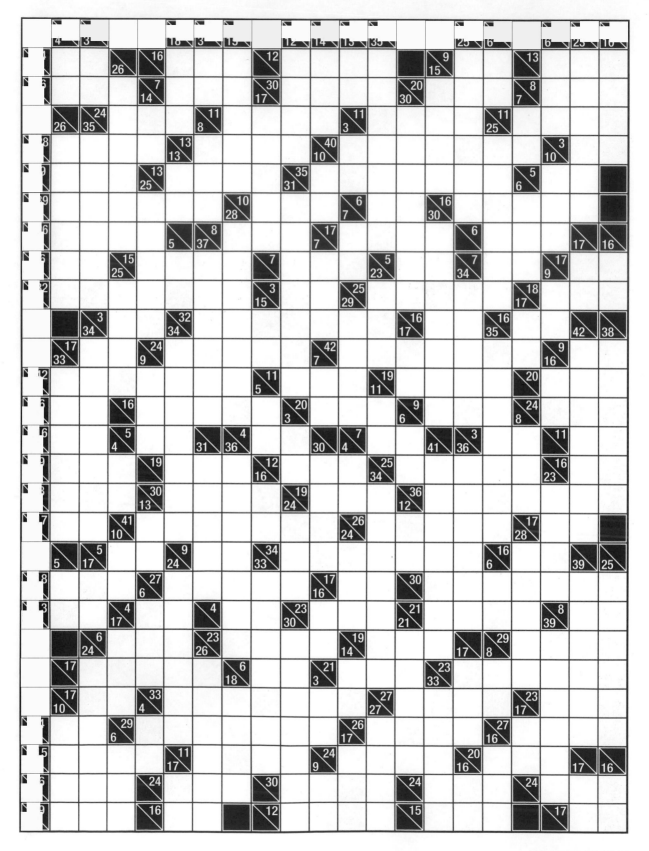

ANSWER, PAGE 79

10

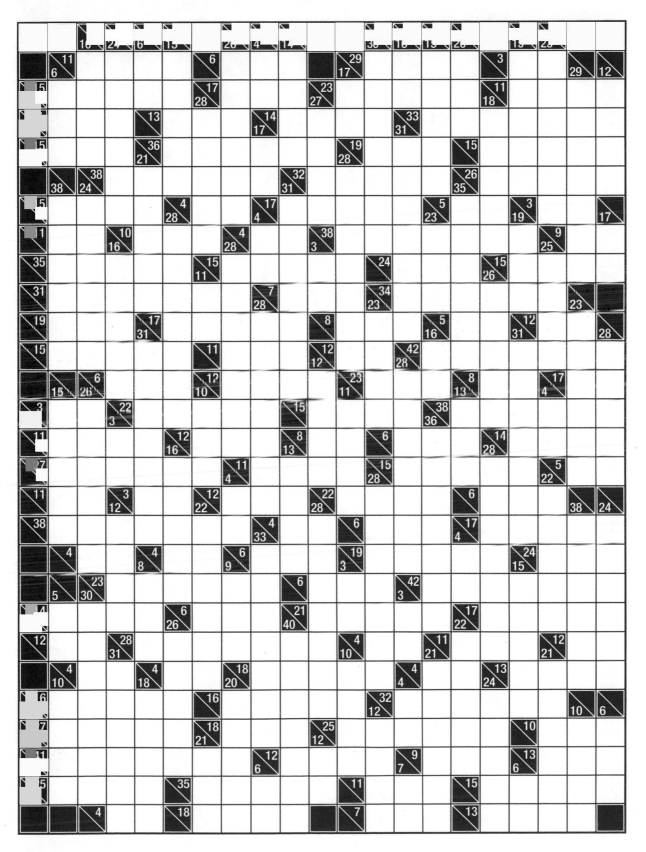

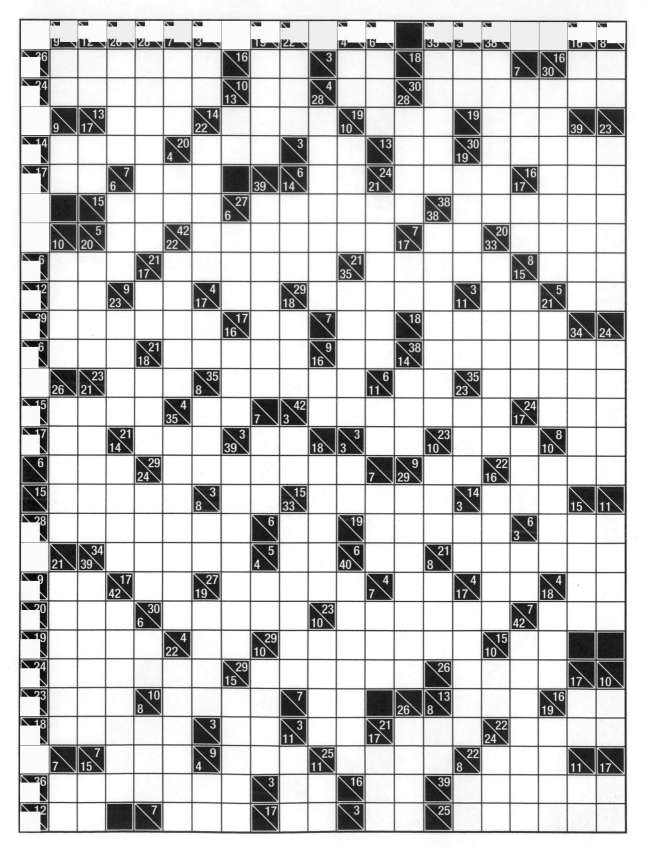

ANSWER, PAGE 80

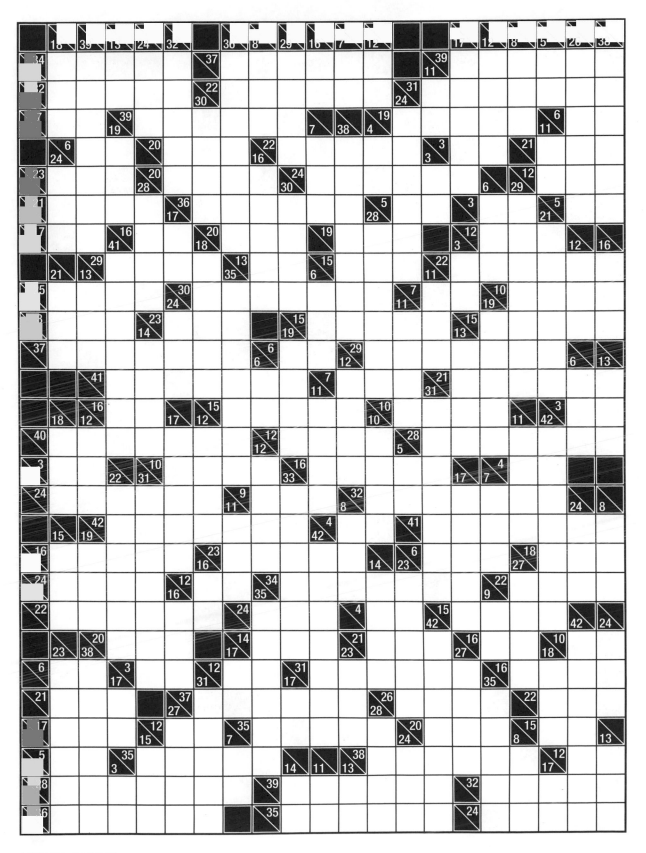

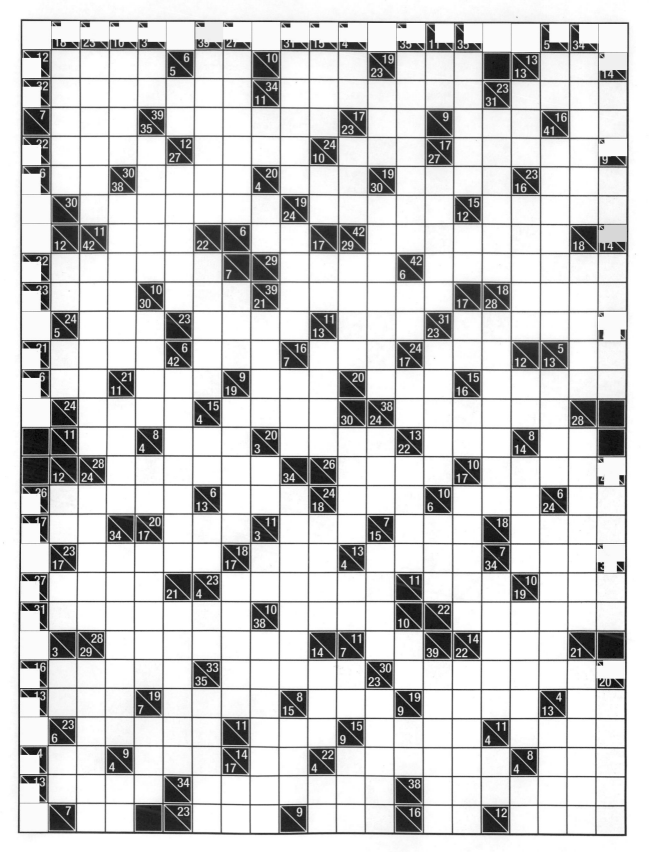

ANSWER, PAGE 80

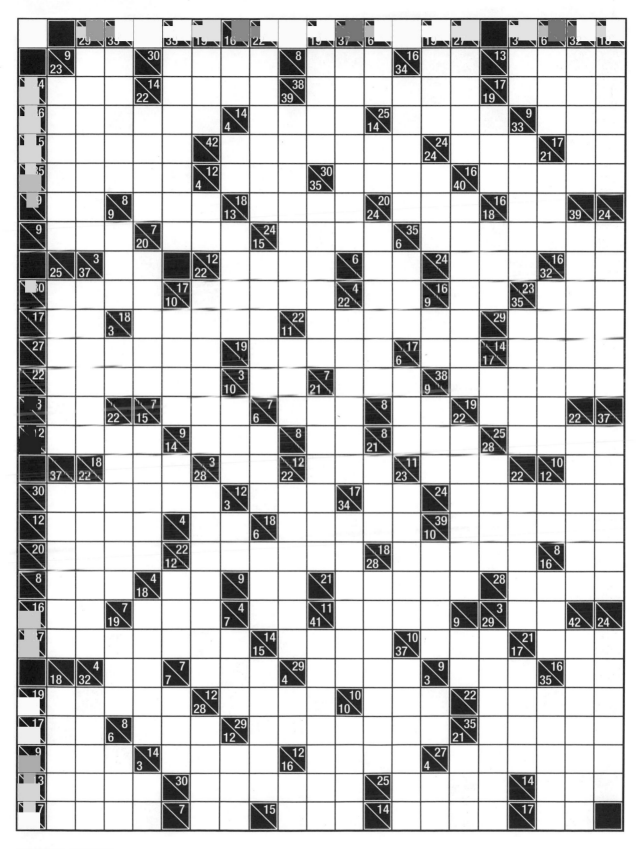

ANSWER, PAGE 81

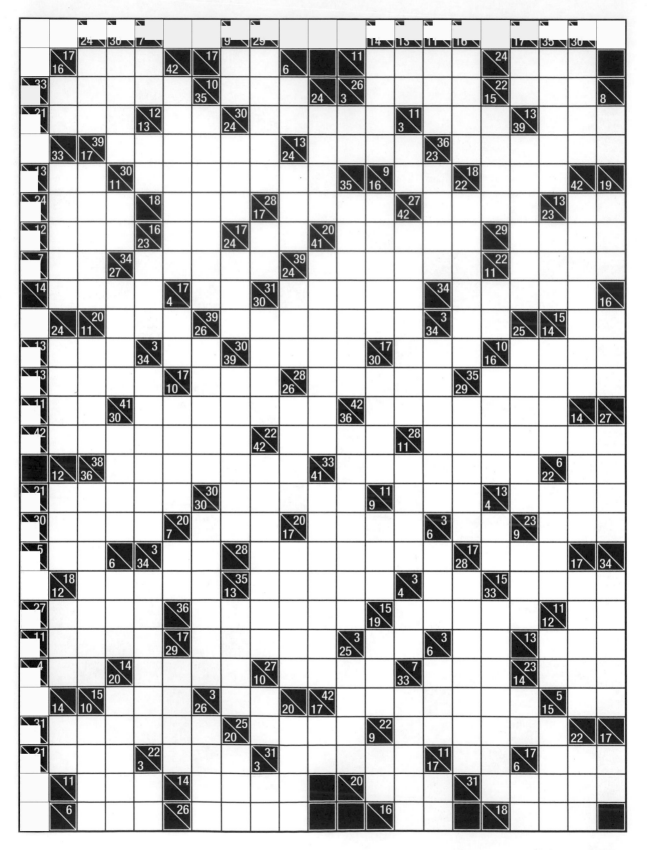

ANSWER, PAGE 81

16

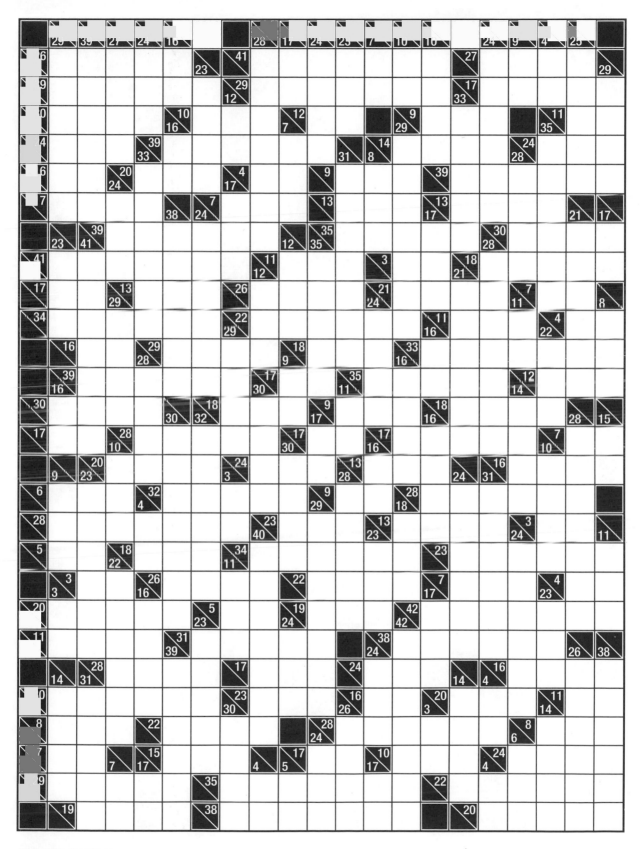

ANSWER, PAGE 81

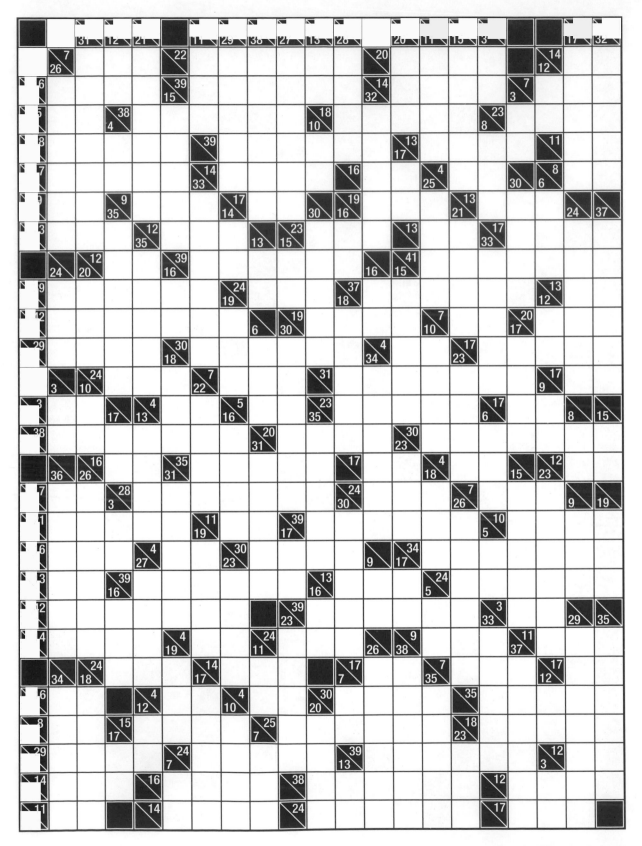

ANSWER, PAGE 81

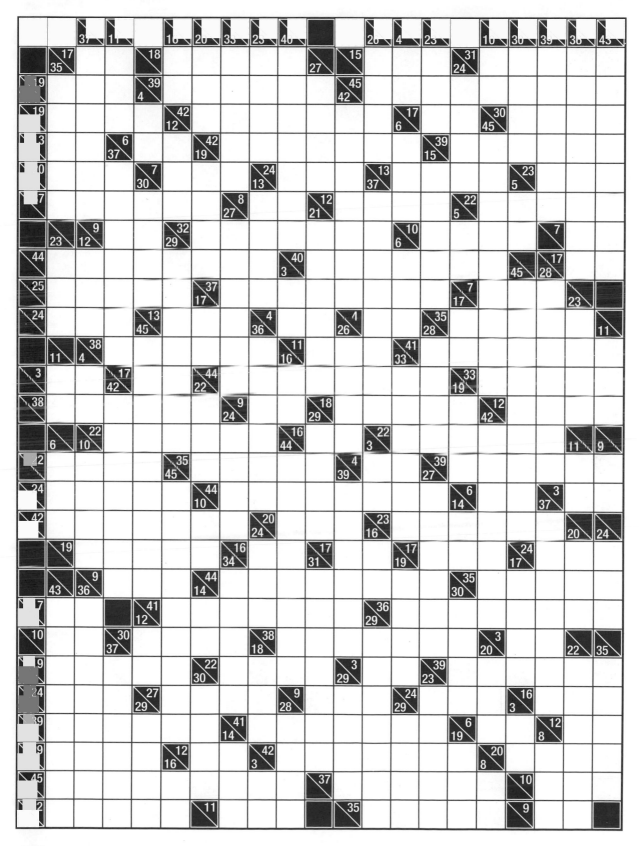

ANSWER, PAGE 82

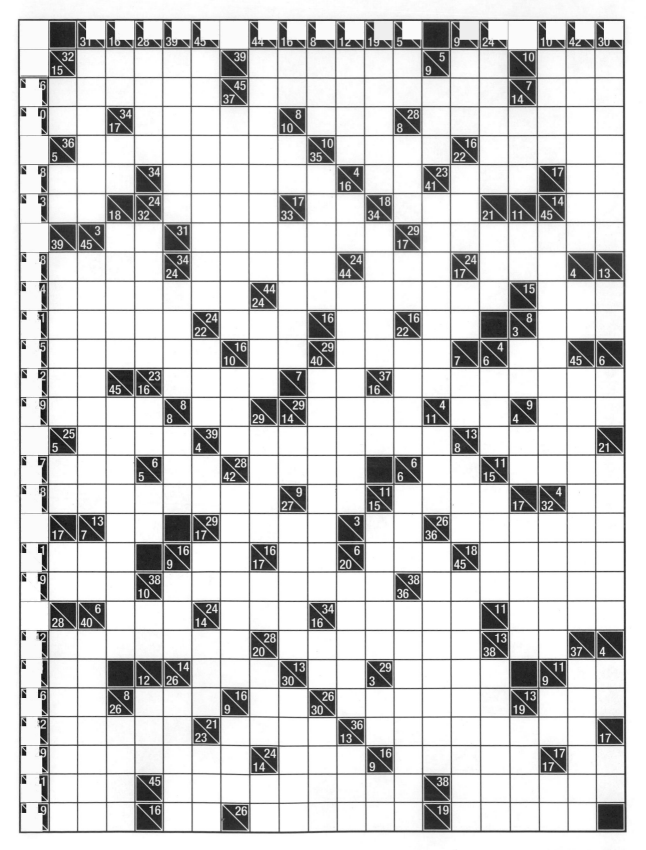

ANSWER, PAGE 82

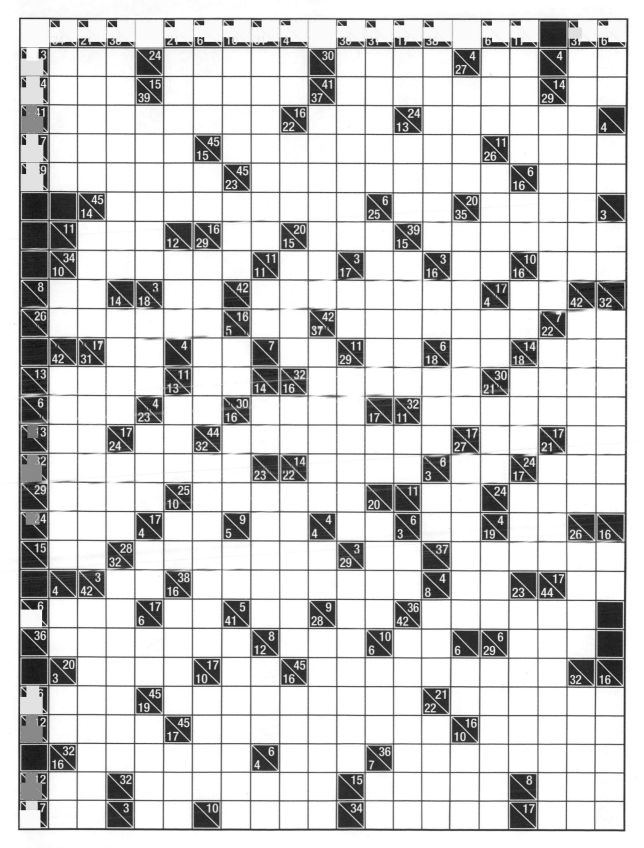

ANSWER, PAGE 82

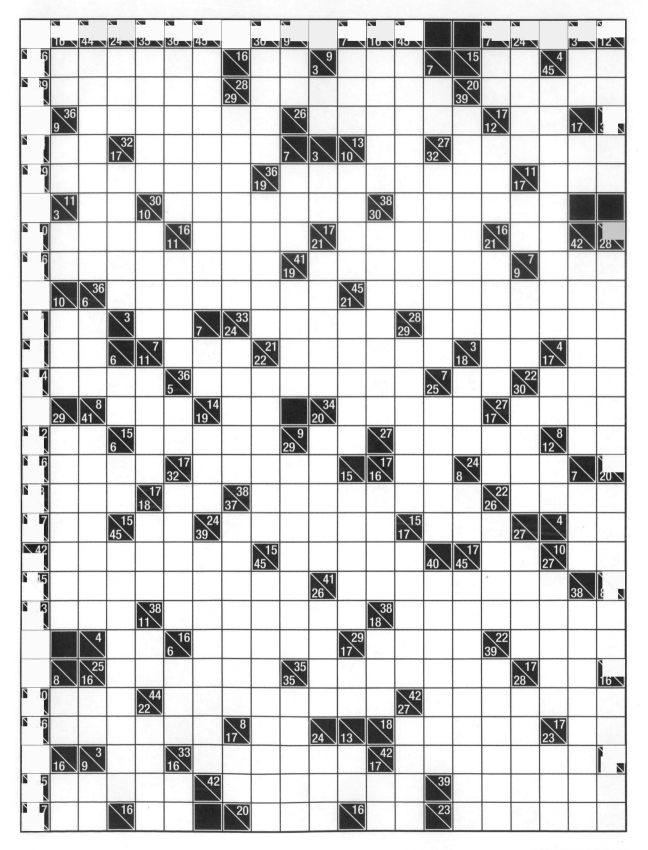

ANSWER, PAGE 82

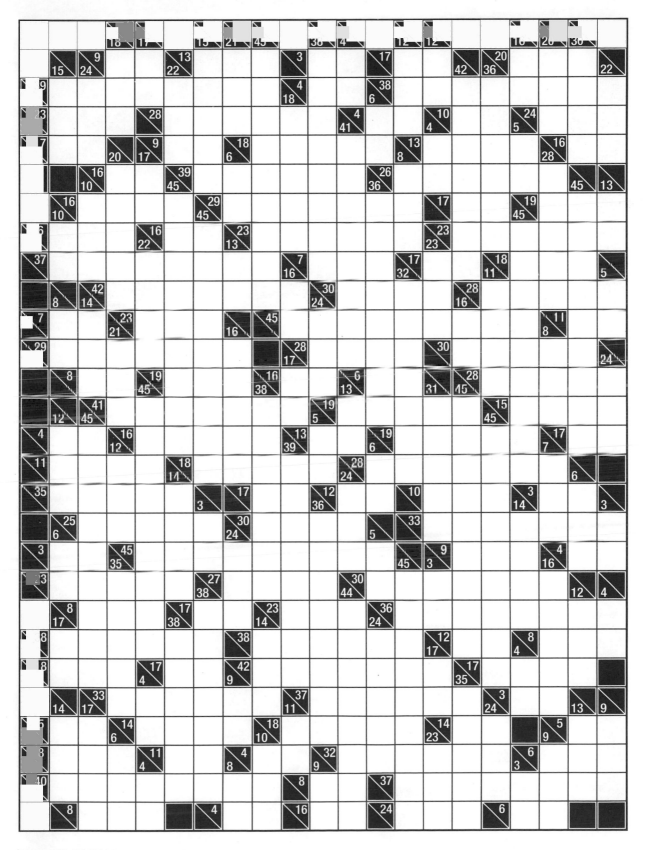

ANSWER, PAGE 83

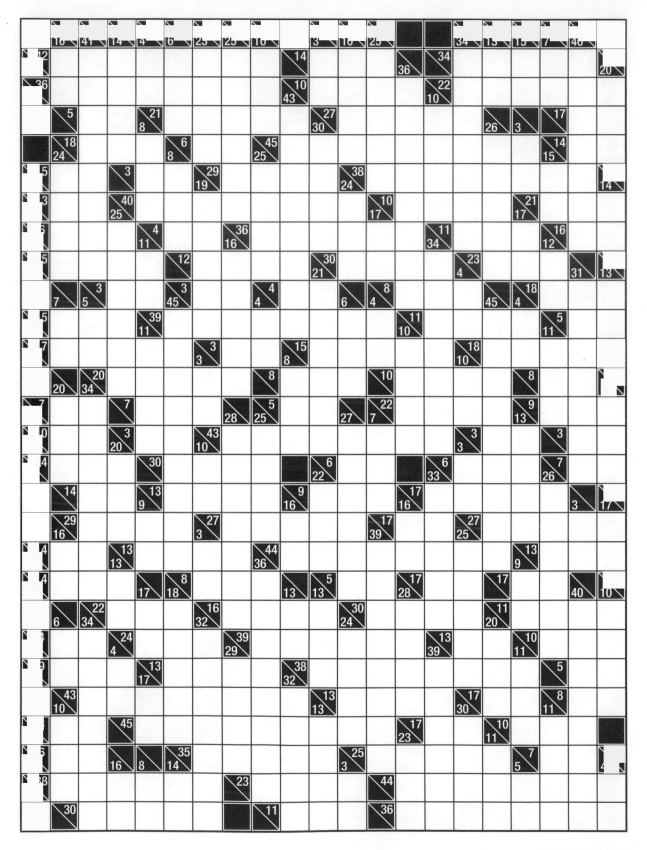

ANSWER, PAGE 83

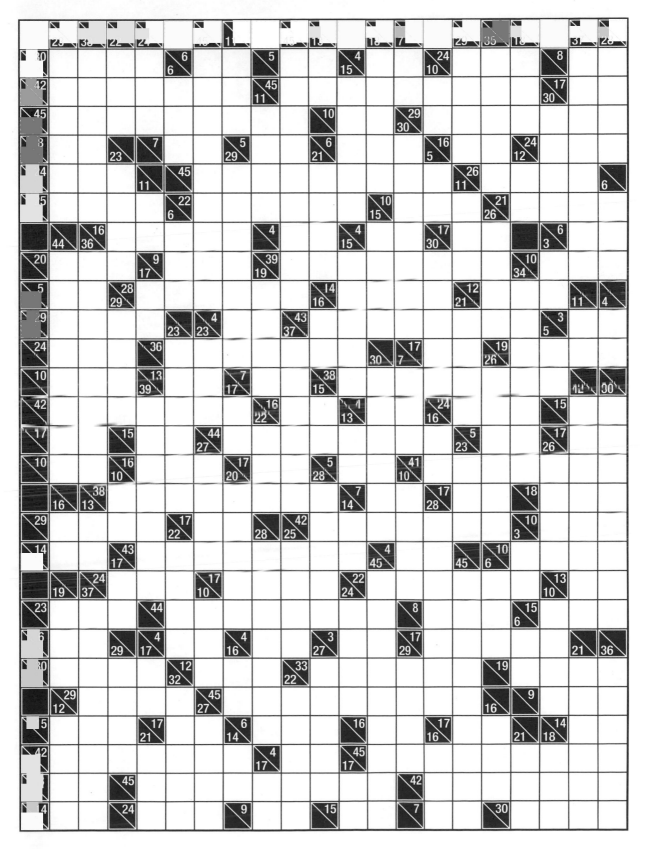

ANSWER, PAGE 83

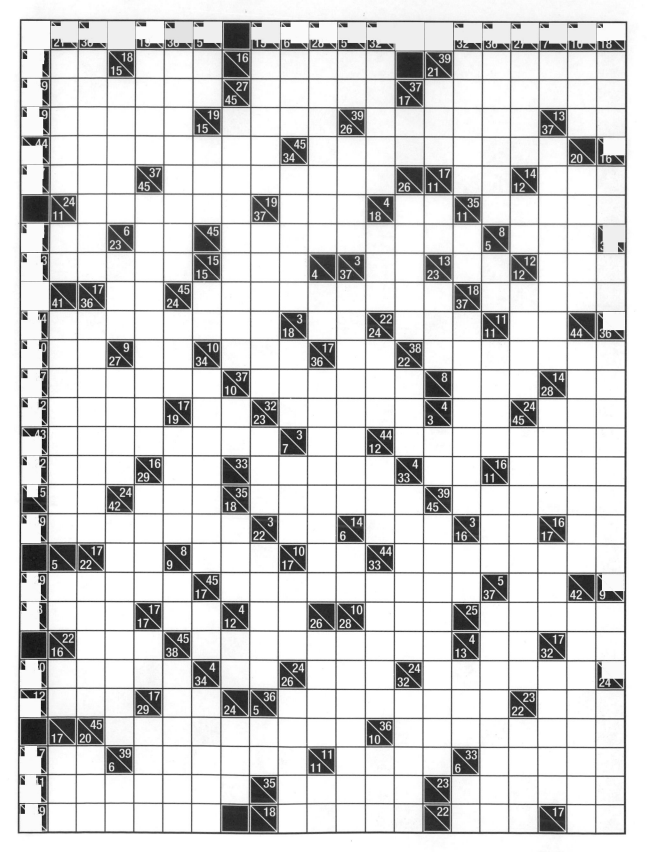

ANSWER, PAGE 83

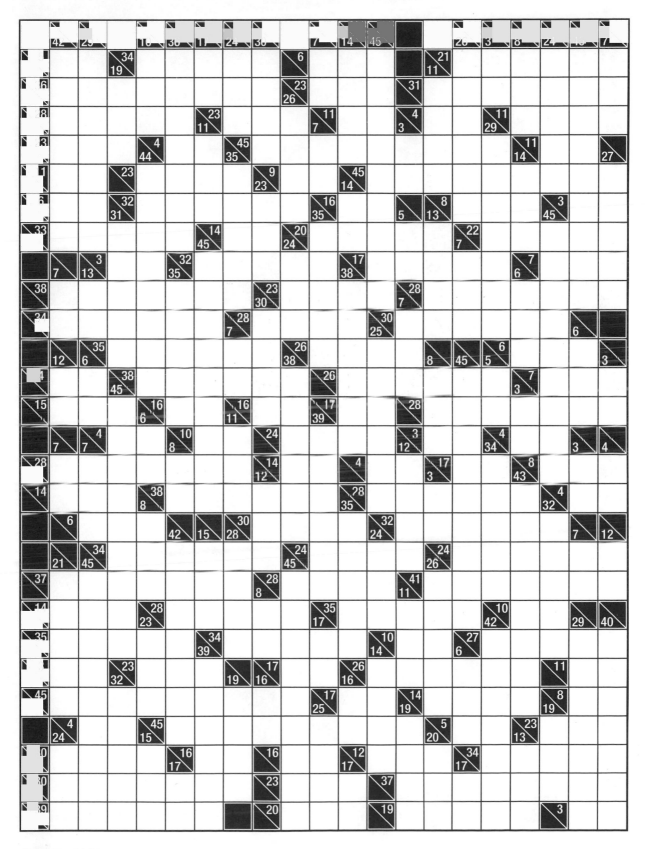

ANSWER, PAGE 84

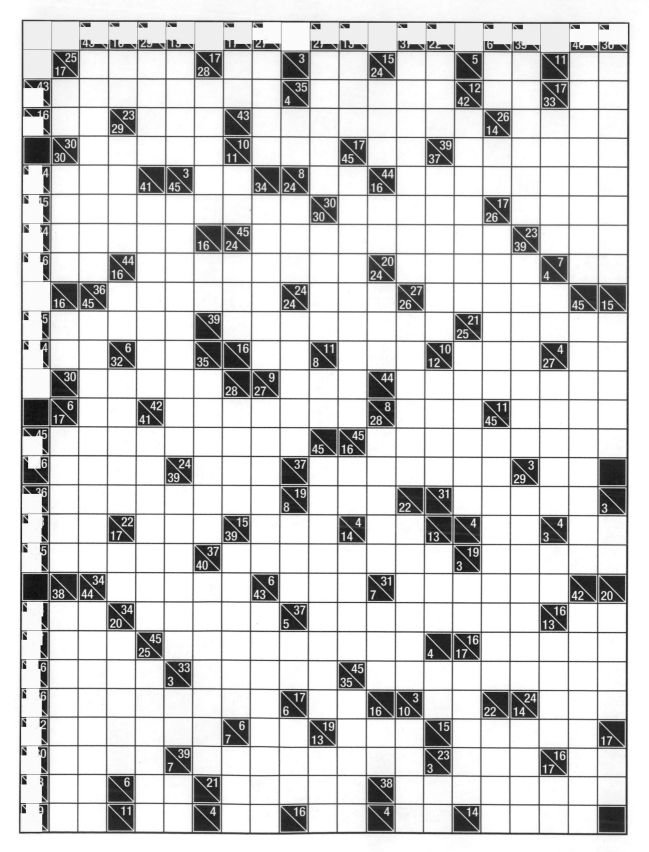

ANSWER, PAGE 84

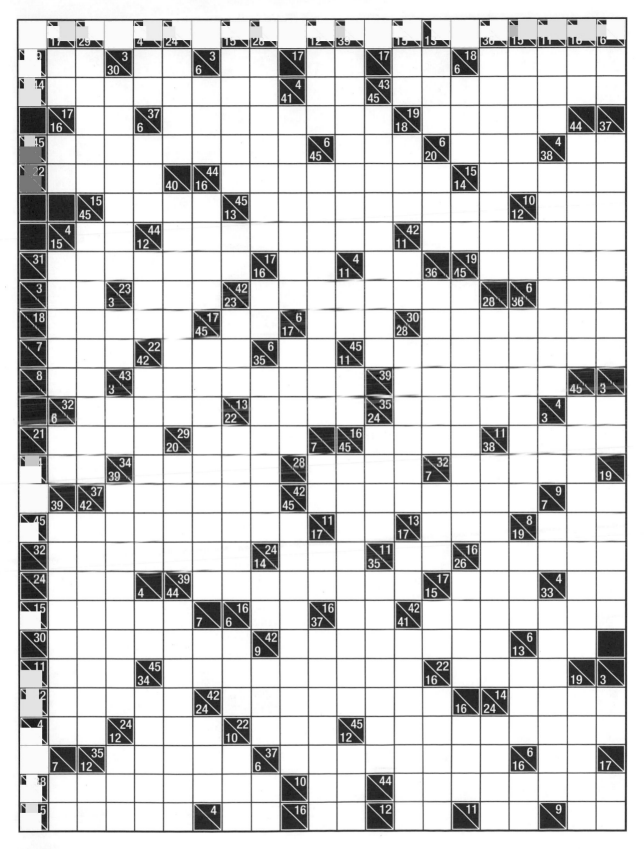

ANSWER, PAGE 84

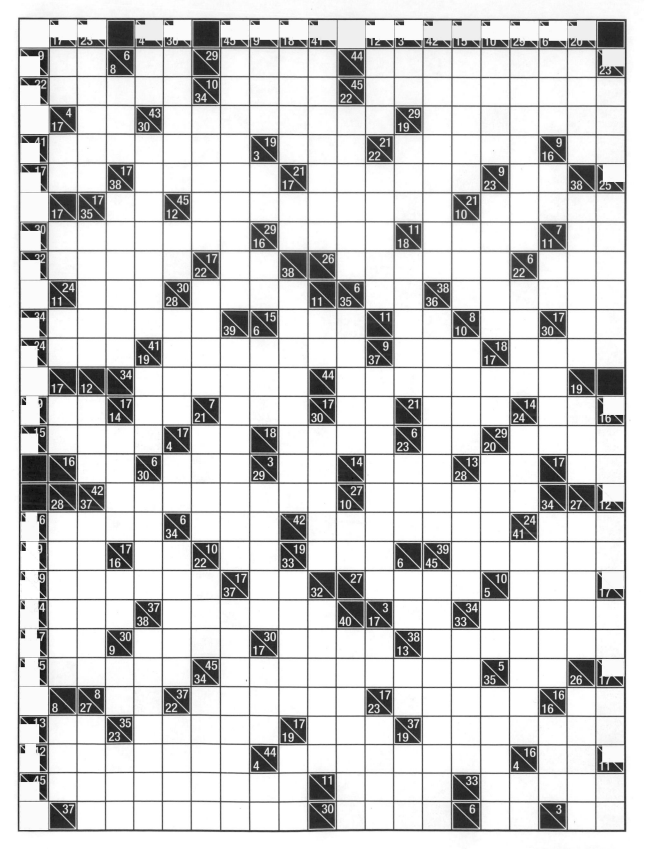

ANSWER, PAGE 84

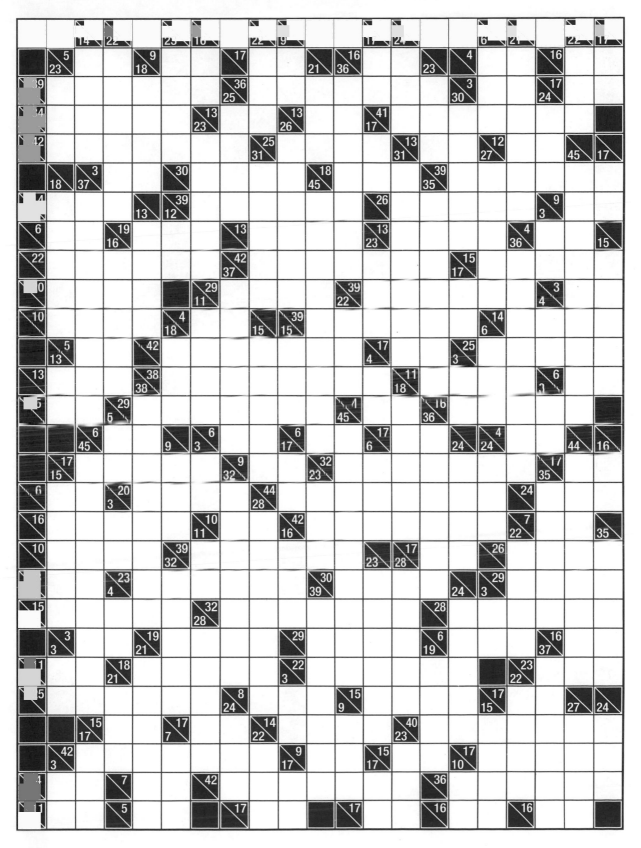

ANSWER, PAGE 85

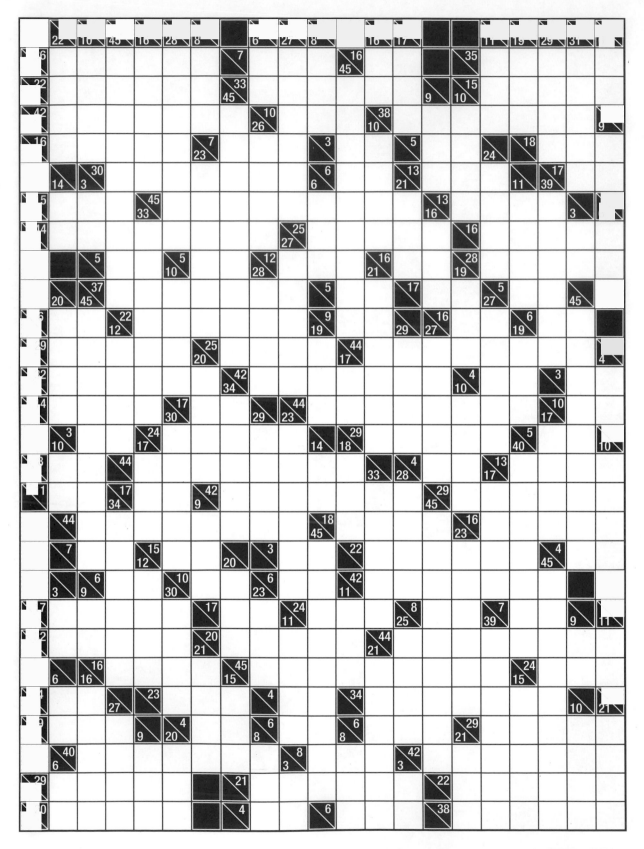

ANSWER, PAGE 85

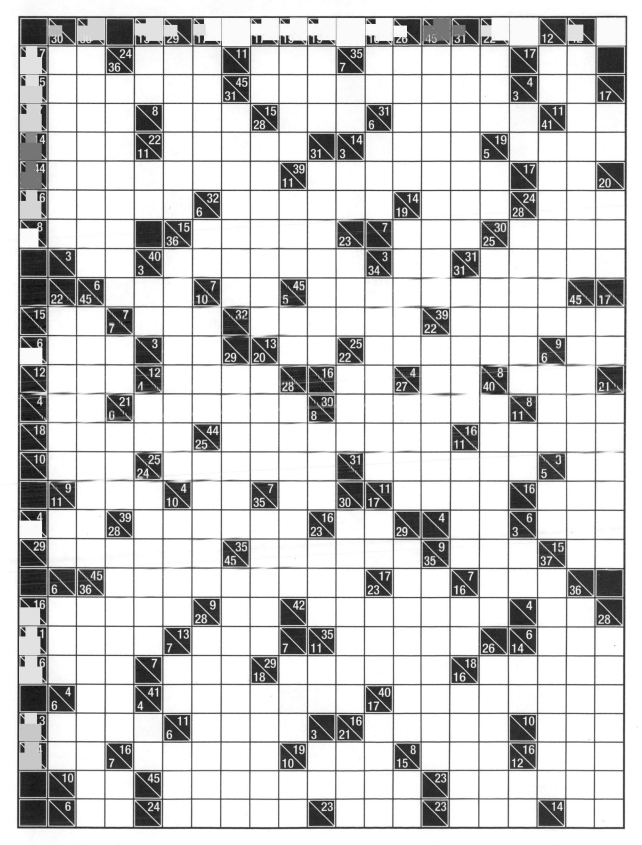

ANSWER, PAGE 85

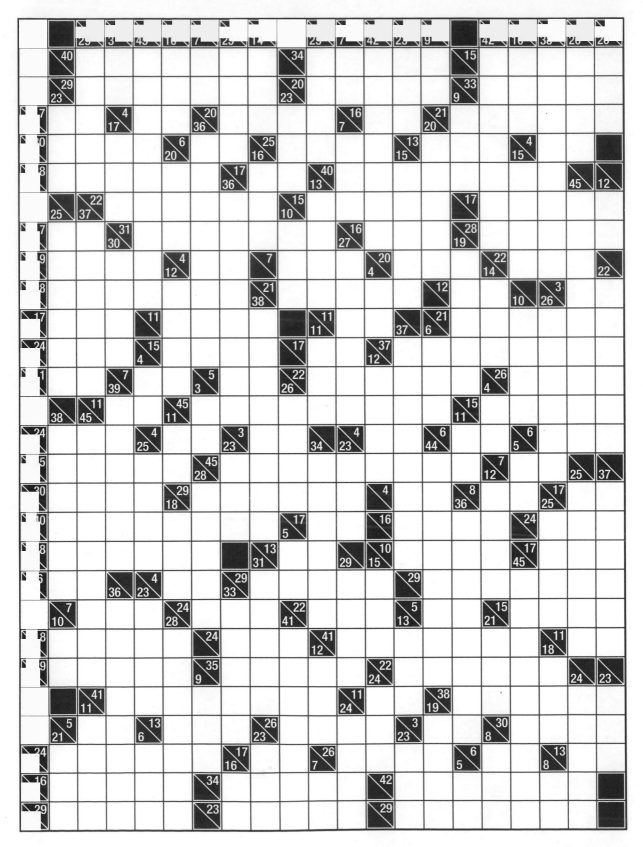

ANSWER, PAGE 85

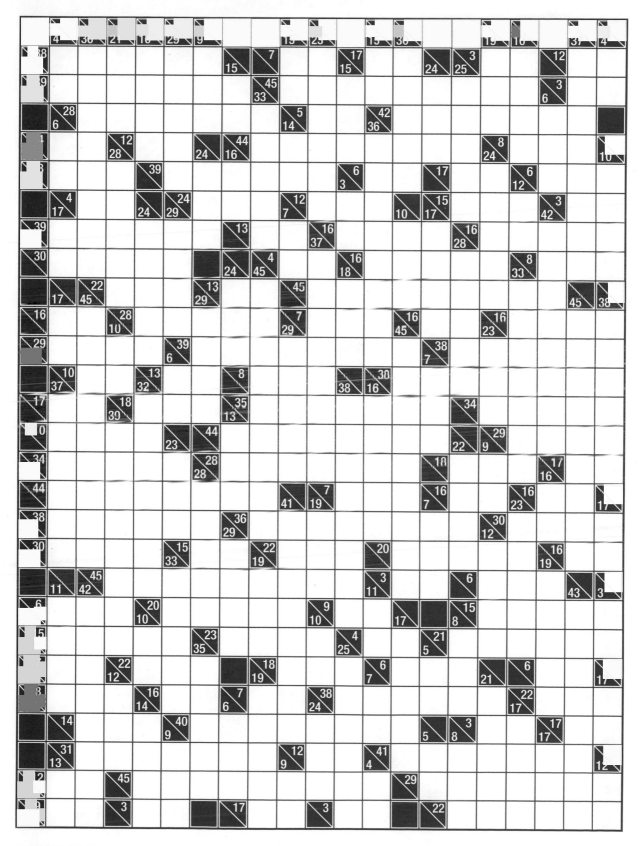

ANSWER, PAGE 86

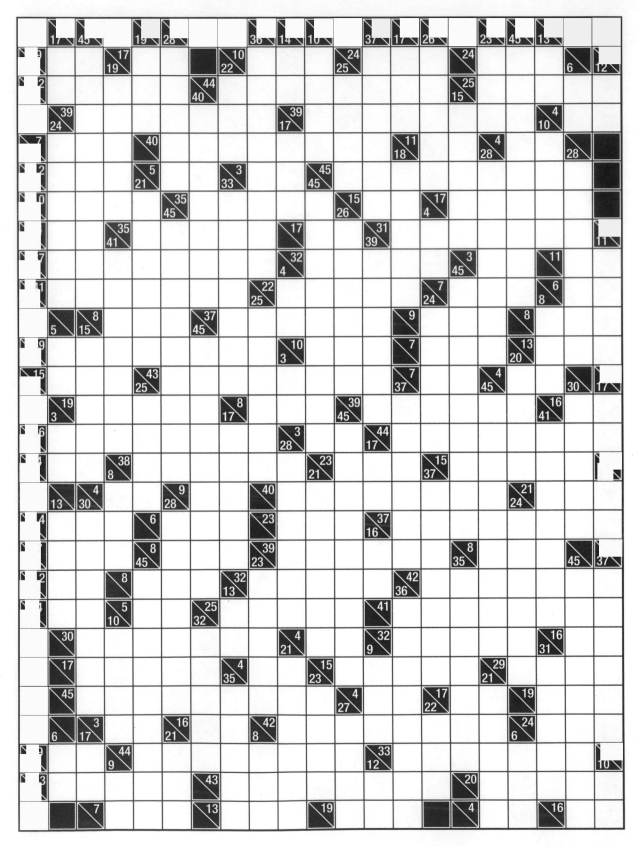

ANSWER, PAGE 86

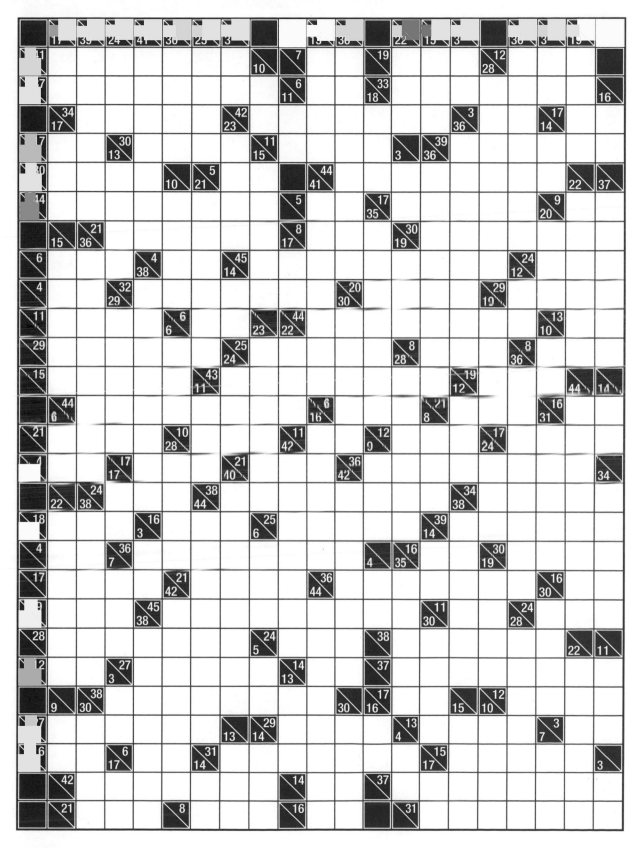

ANSWER, PAGE 86

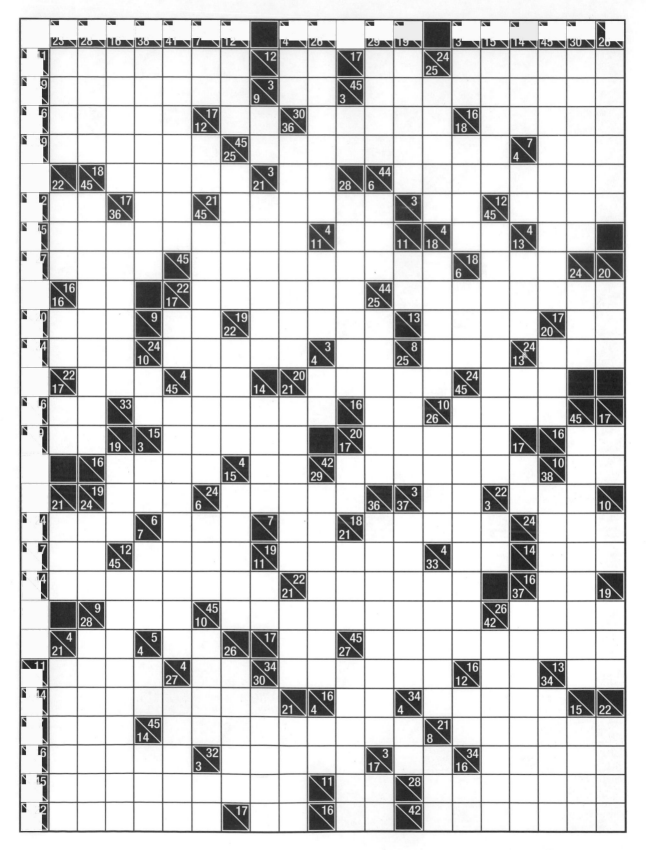

ANSWER, PAGE 86

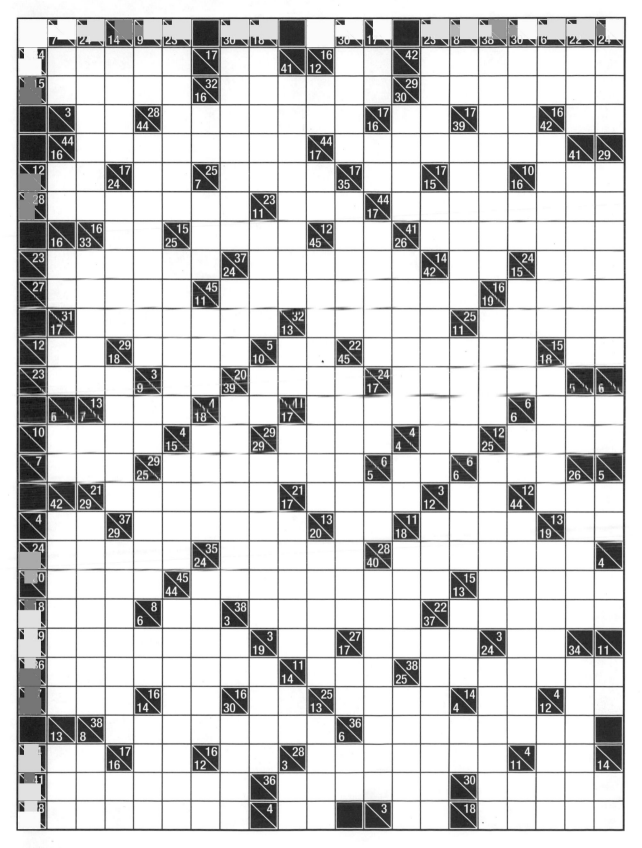

ANSWER, PAGE 87

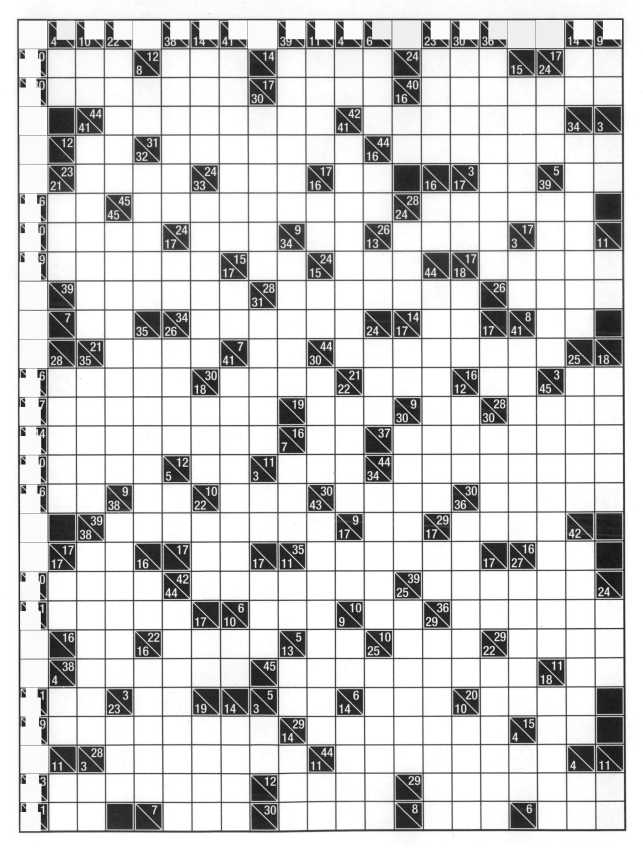

ANSWER, PAGE 87

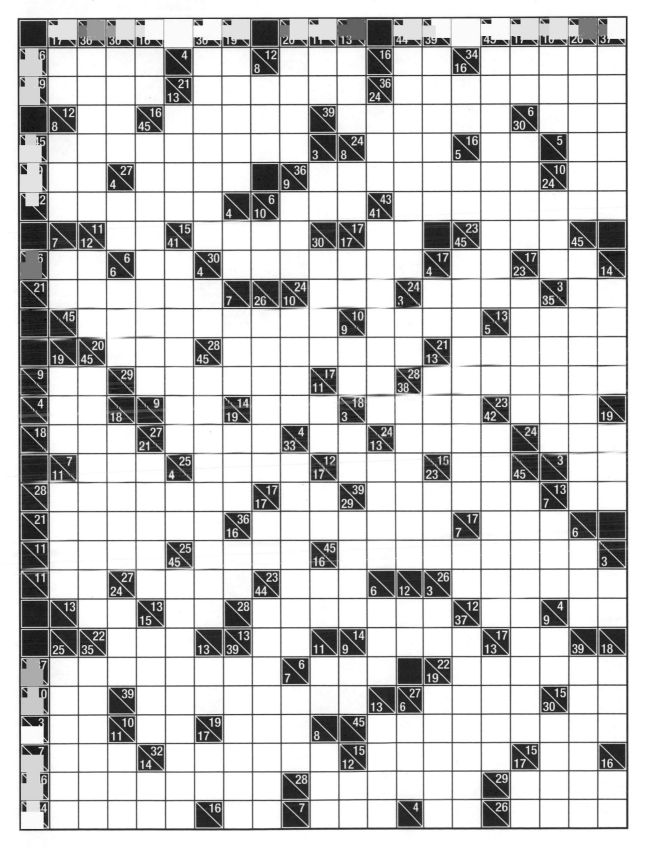

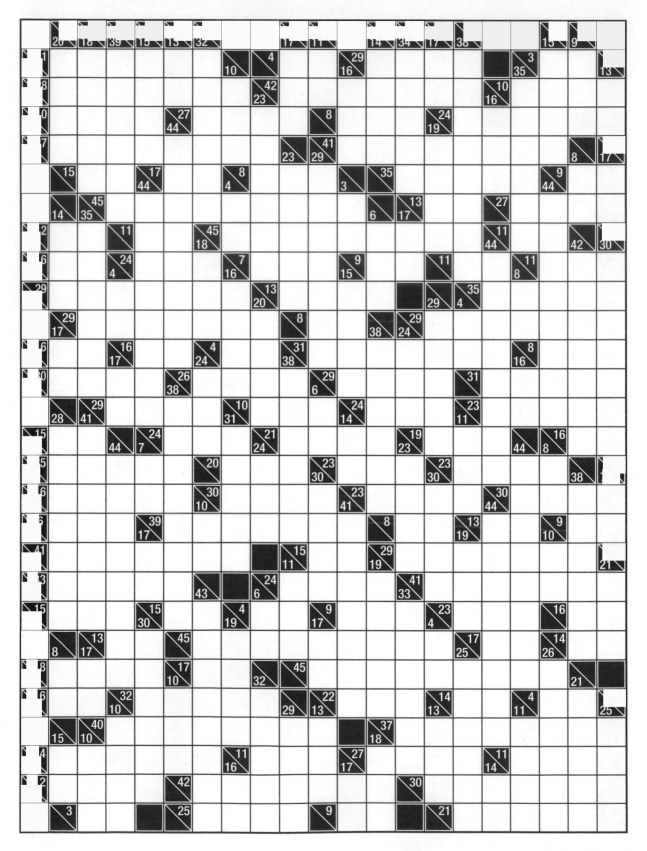

ANSWER, PAGE 87

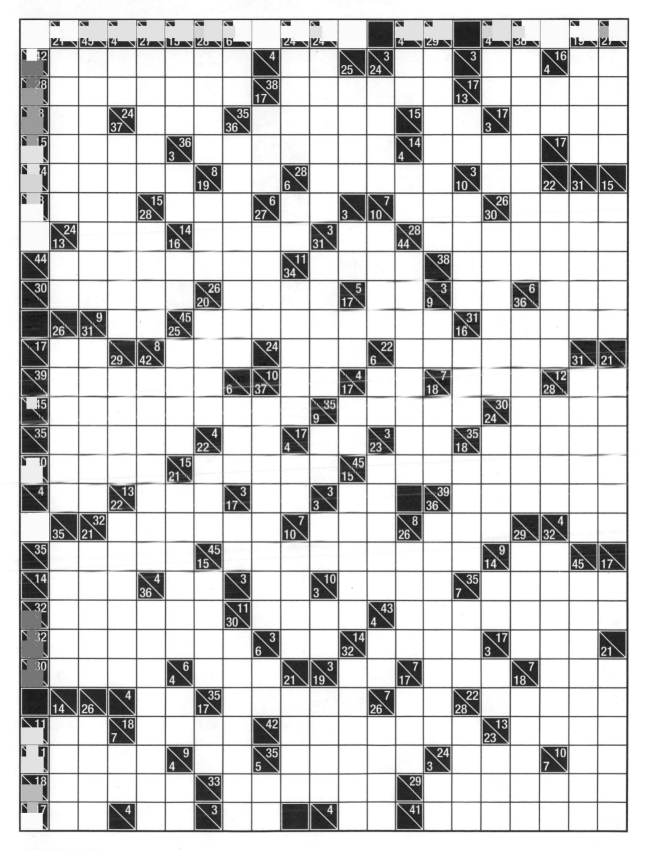

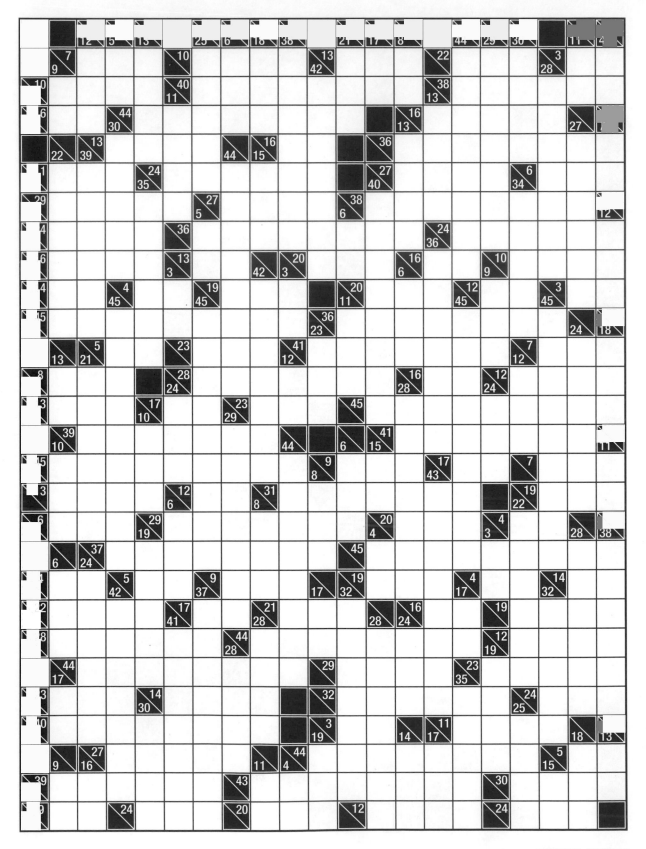

ANSWER, PAGE 88

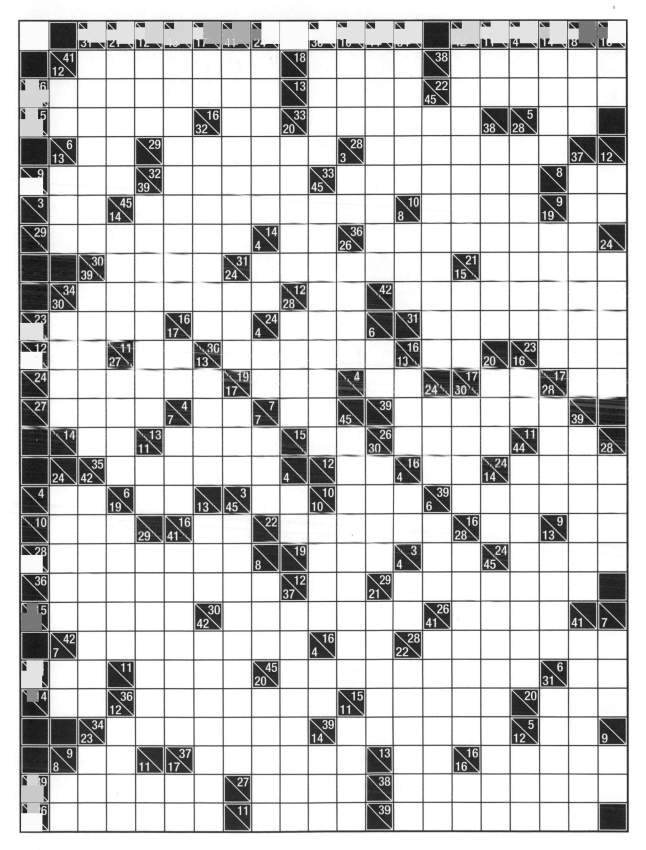

ANSWER, PAGE 88

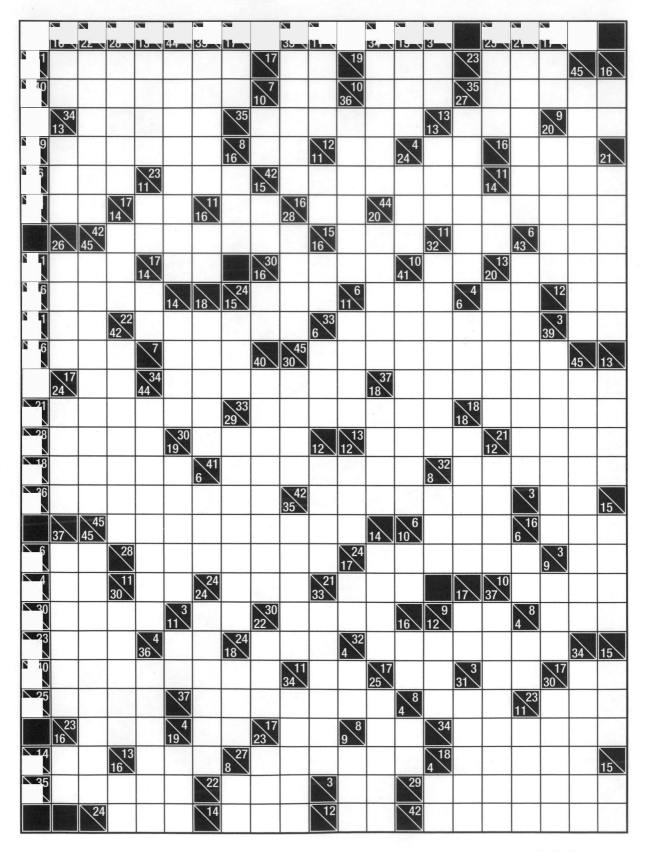

ANSWER, PAGE 88

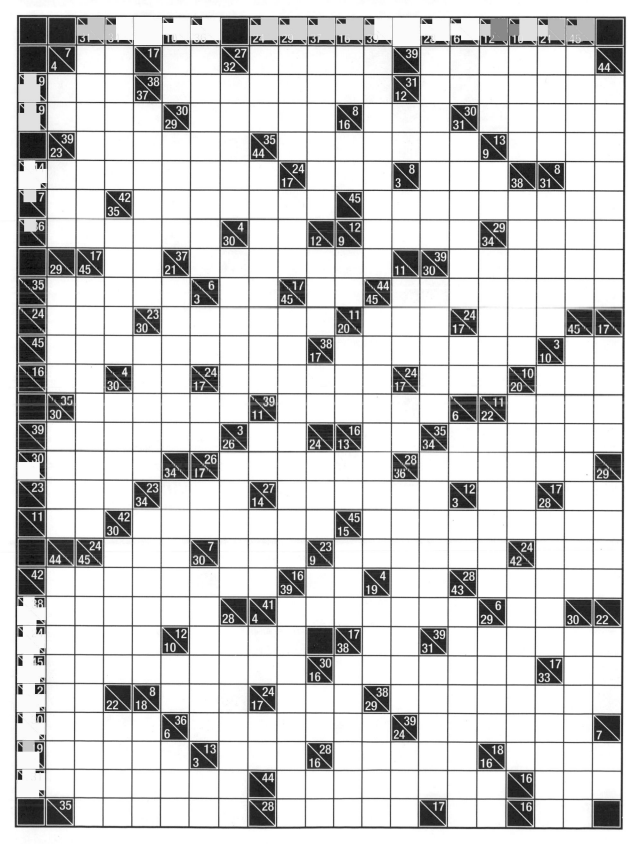

ANSWER, PAGE 89

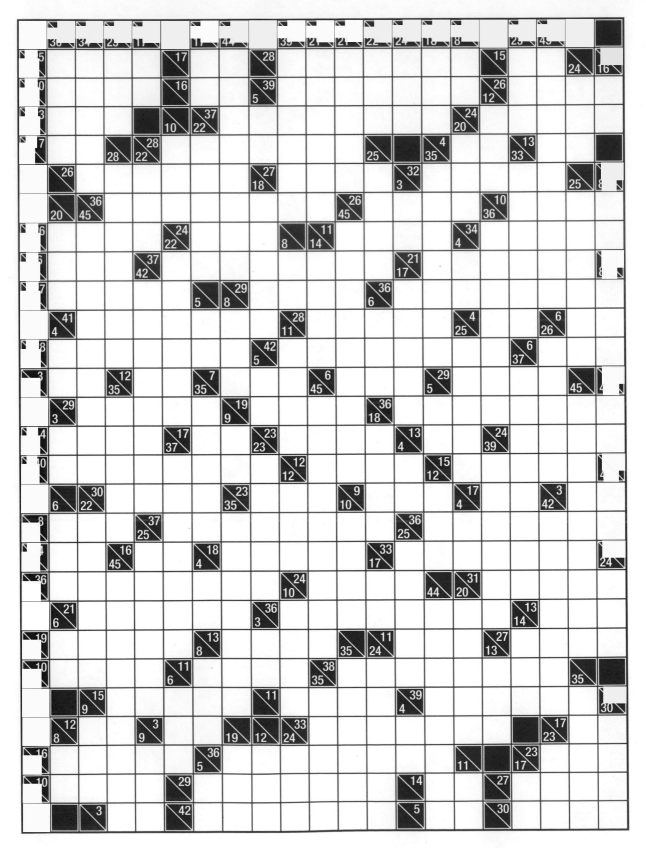

ANSWER, PAGE 89

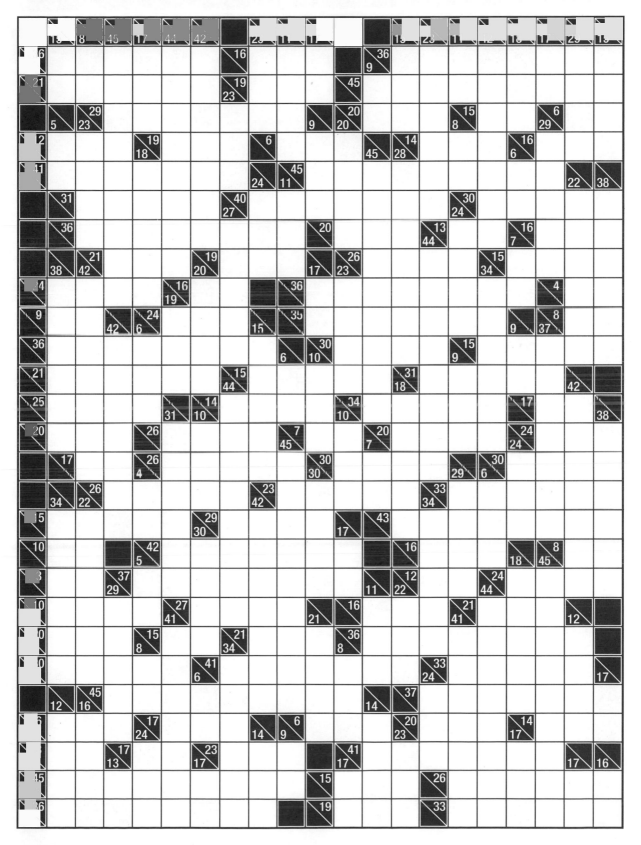

ANSWER, PAGE 89

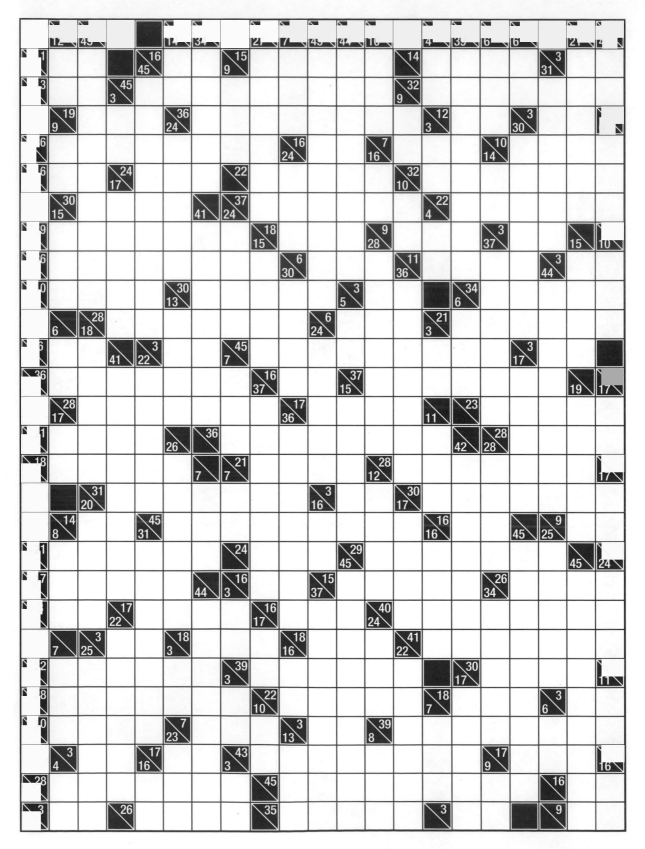

ANSWER, PAGE 89

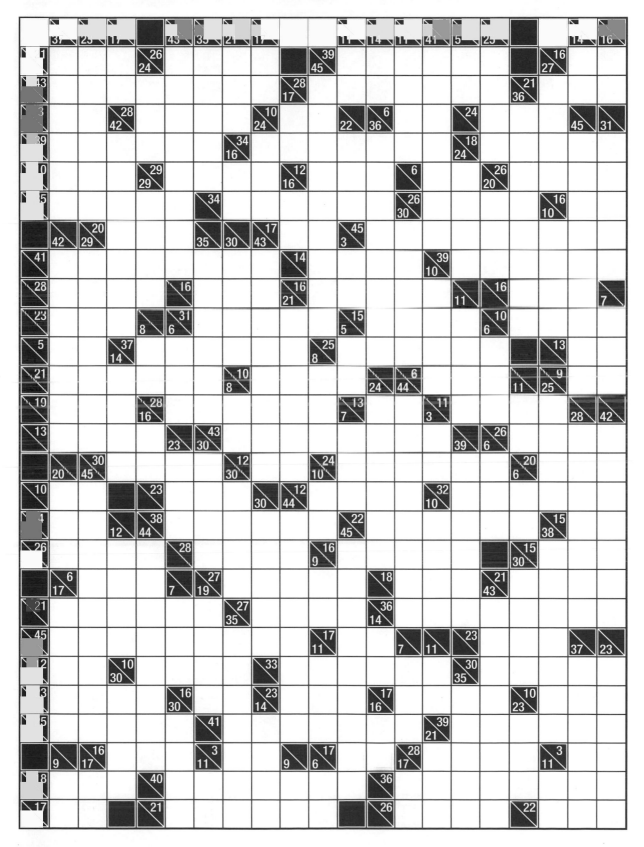

ANSWER, PAGE 90

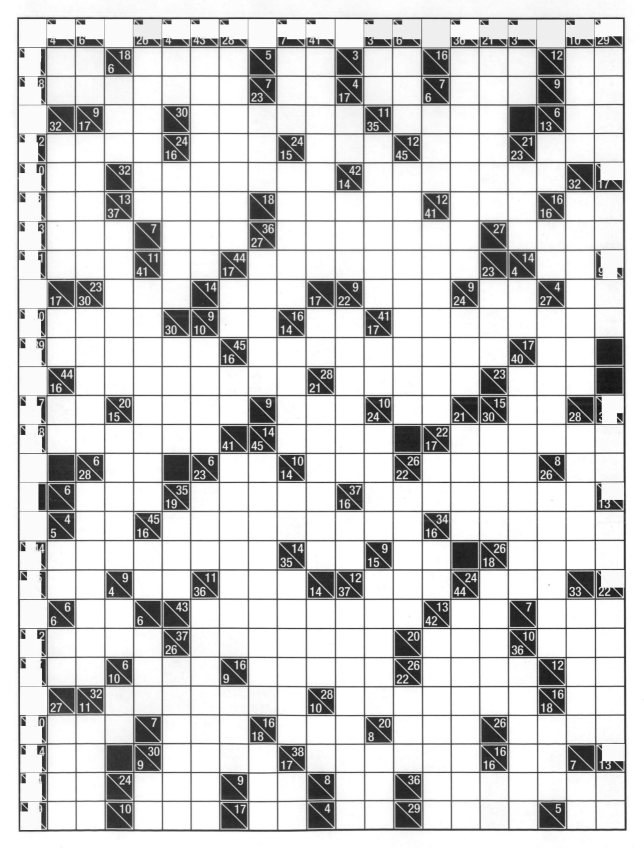

ANSWER, PAGE 90

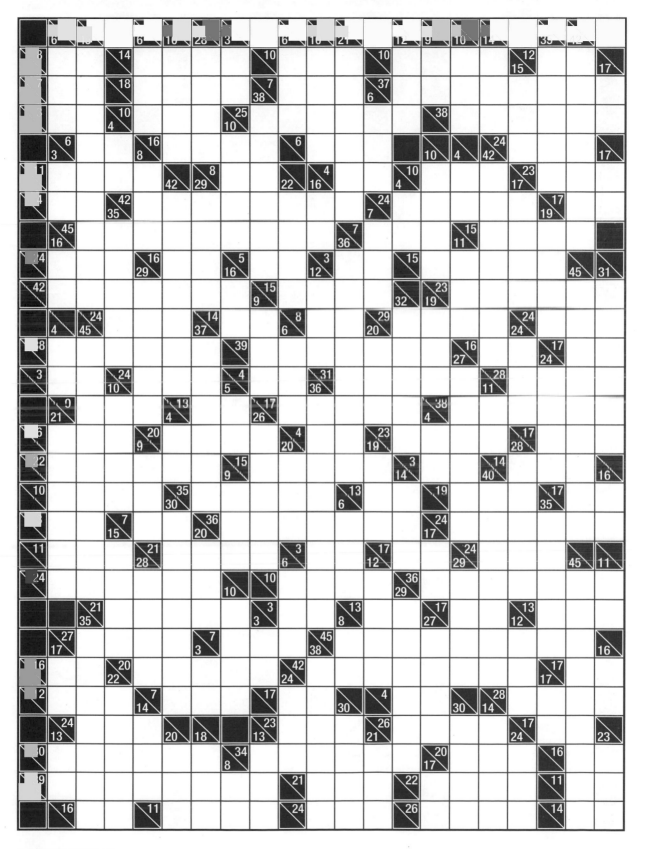

ANSWER, PAGE 90

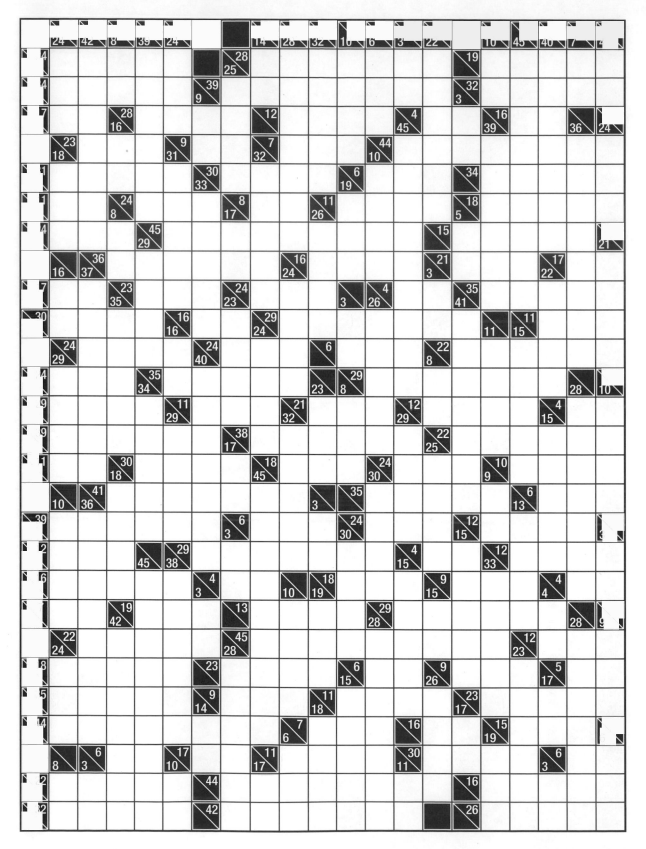

ANSWER, PAGE 90

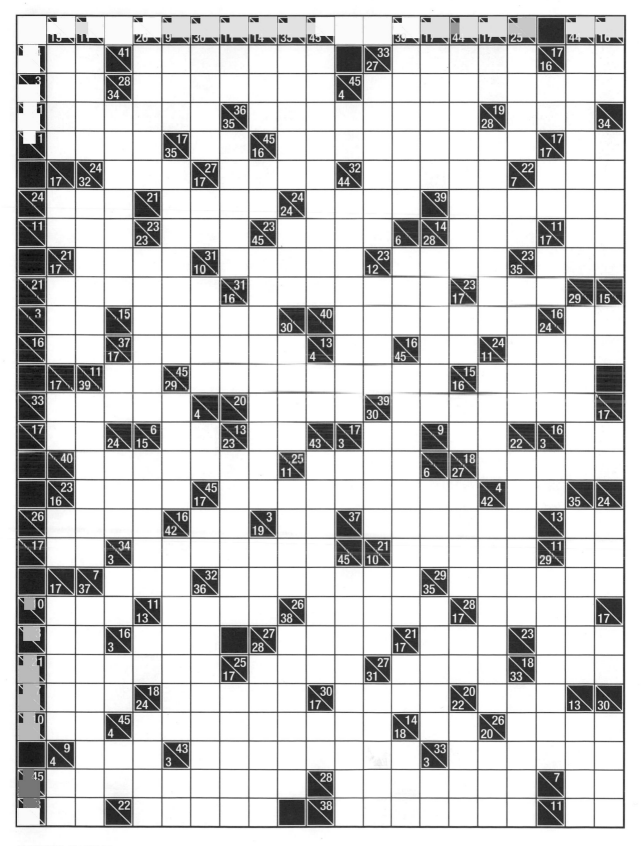

ANSWER, PAGE 91

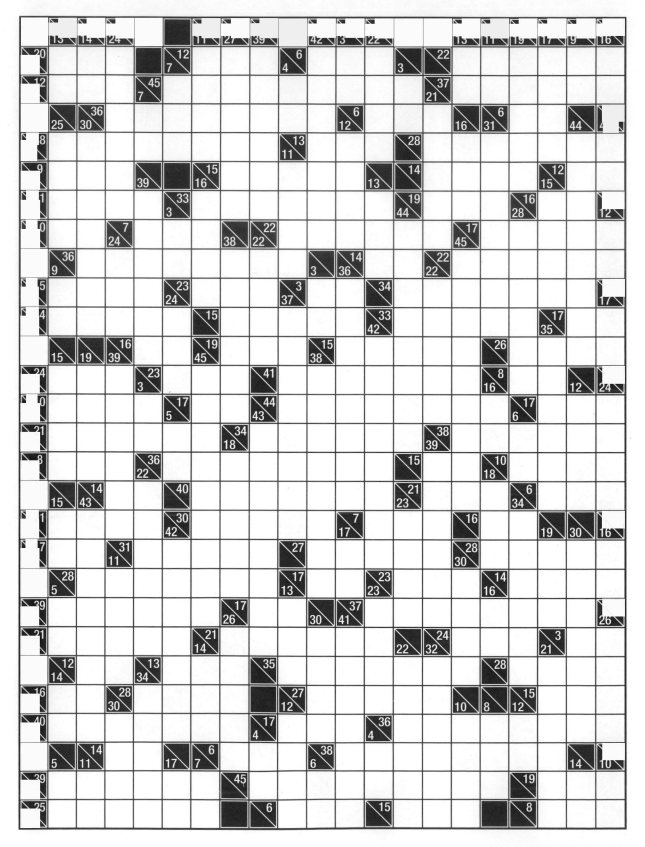

ANSWER, PAGE 91

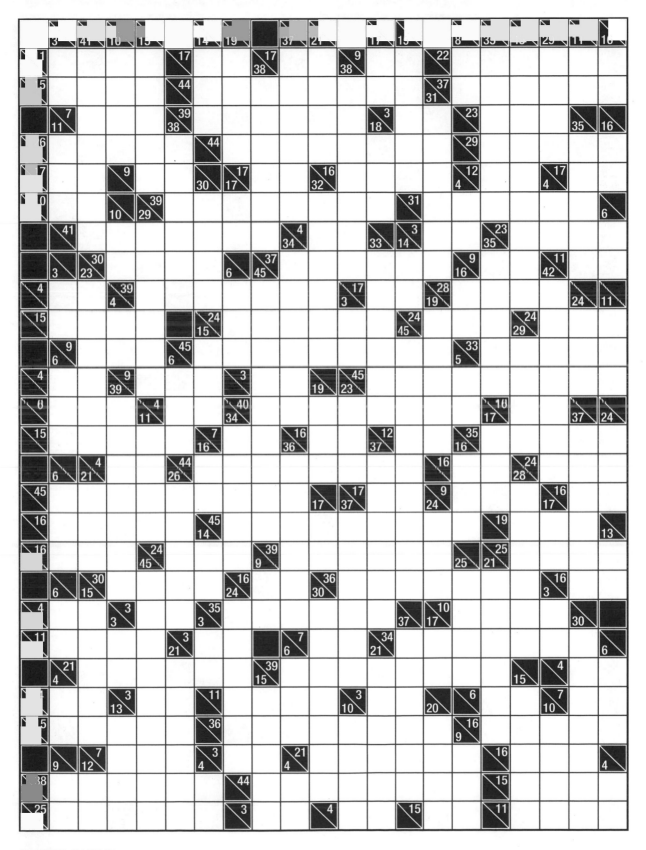

ANSWER, PAGE 91

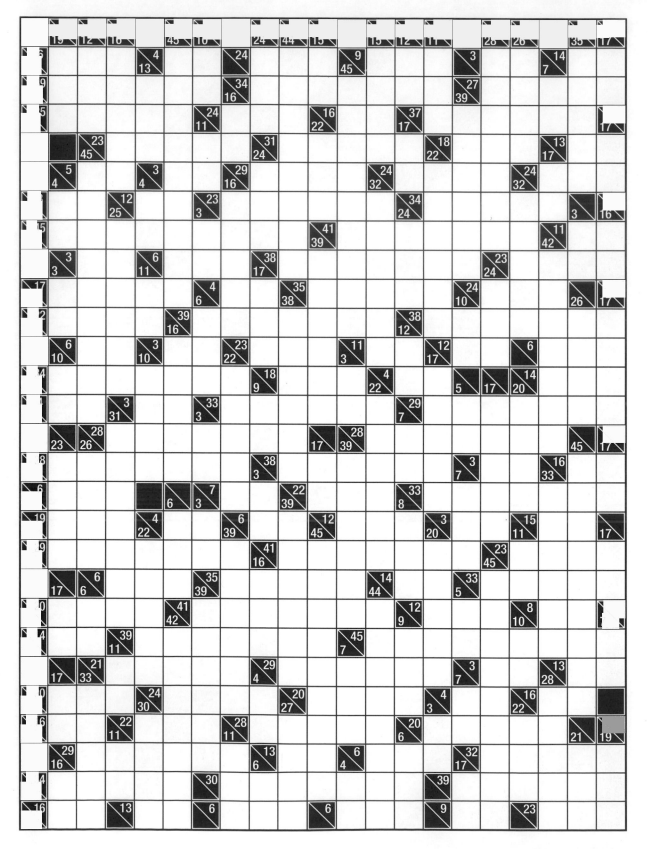

ANSWER, PAGE 91

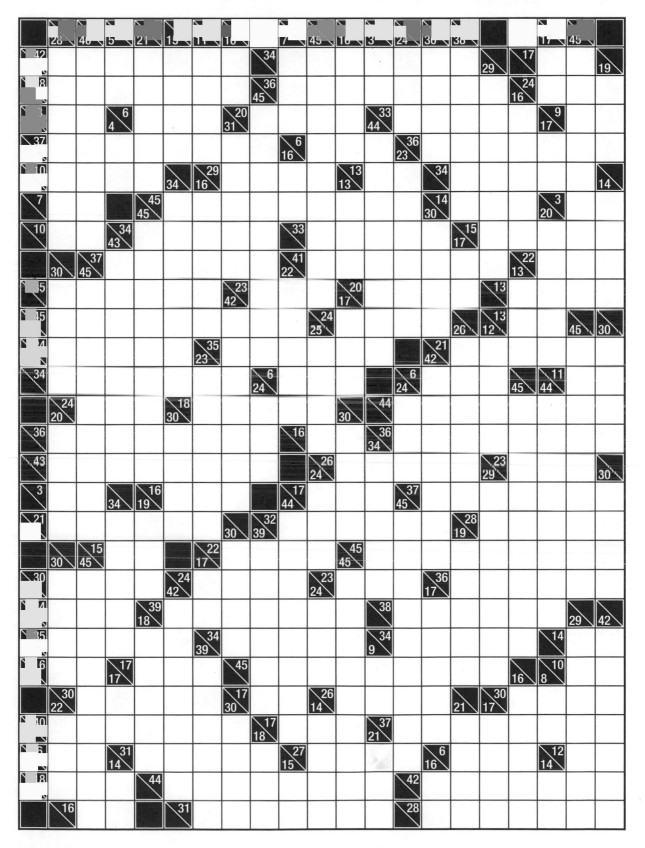

ANSWER, PAGE 92

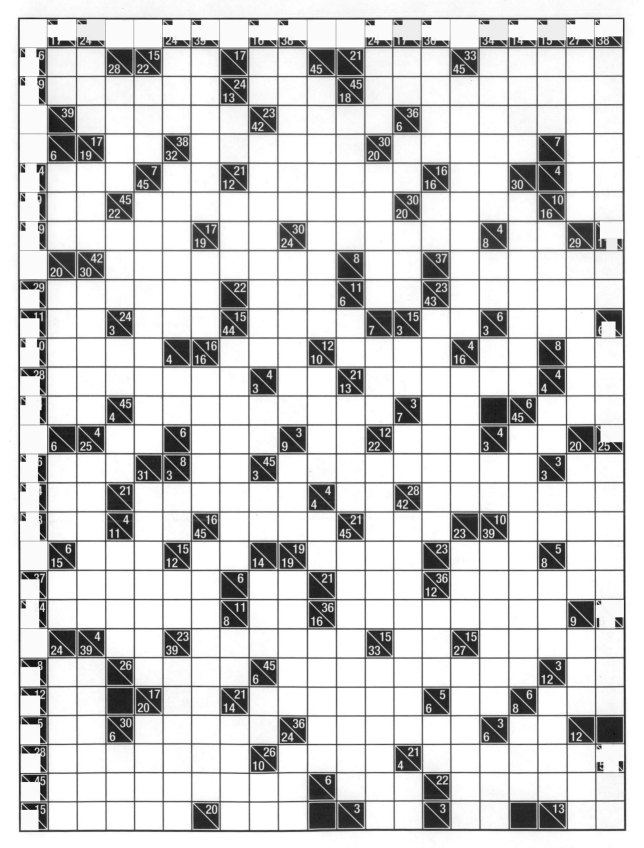

ANSWER, PAGE 92

60

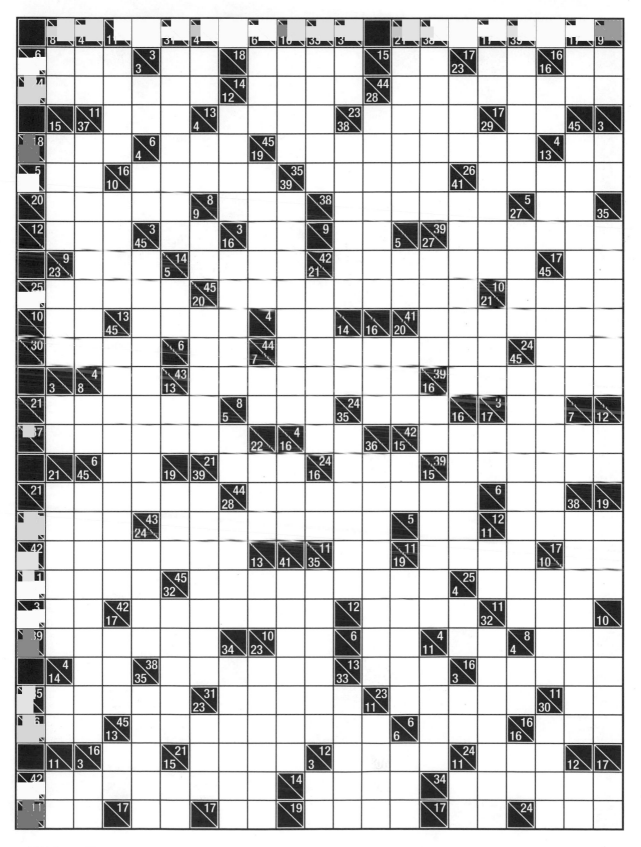

ANSWER, PAGE 92

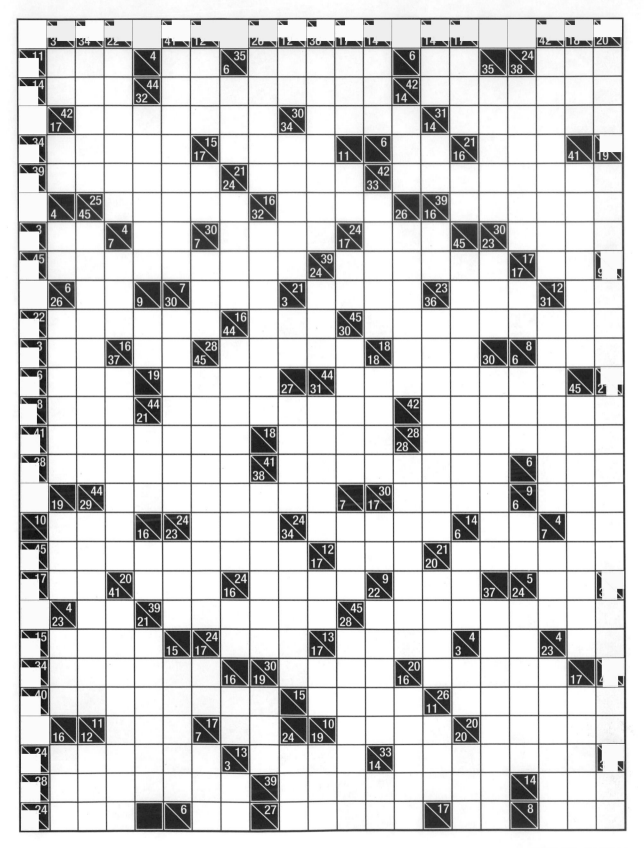

ANSWER, PAGE 92

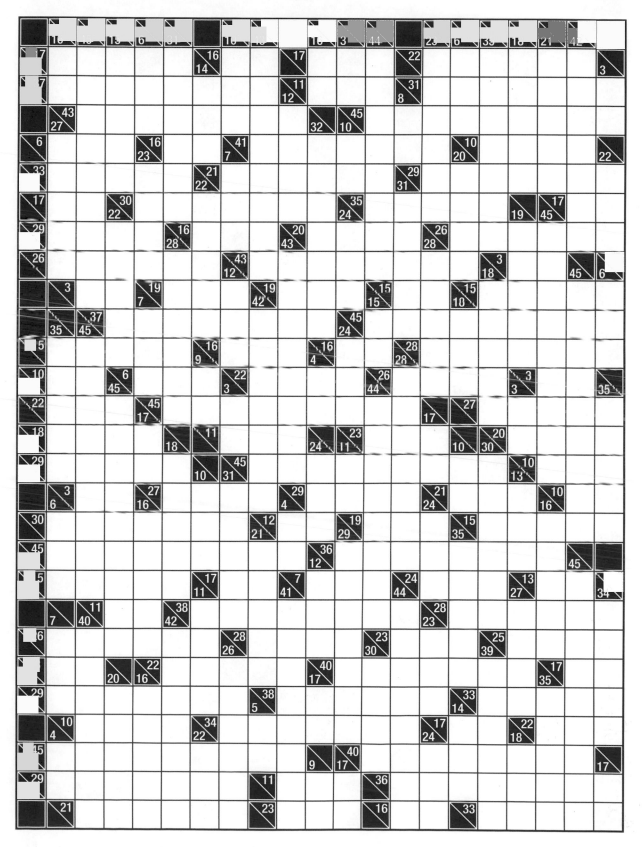

ANSWER, PAGE 93

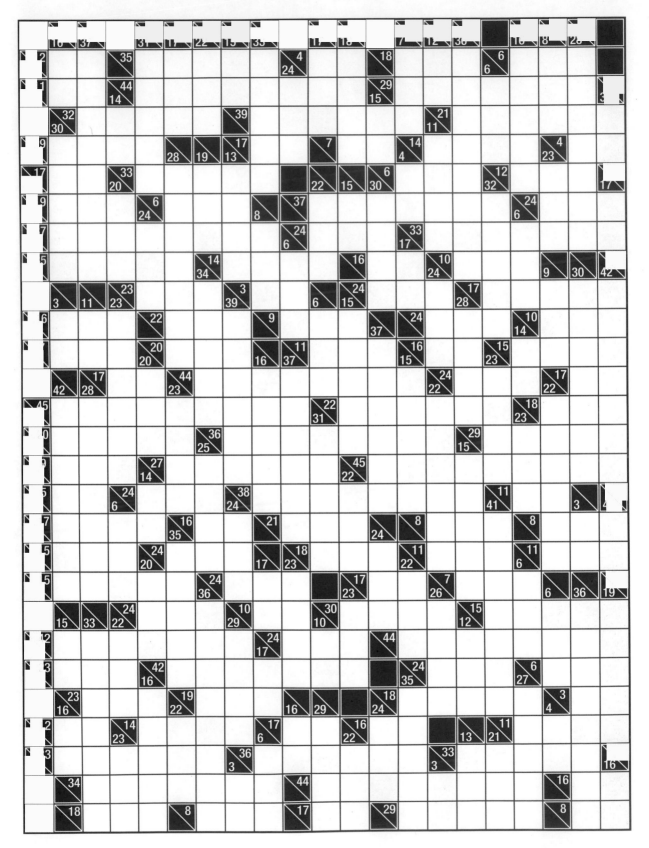

ANSWER, PAGE 93

64

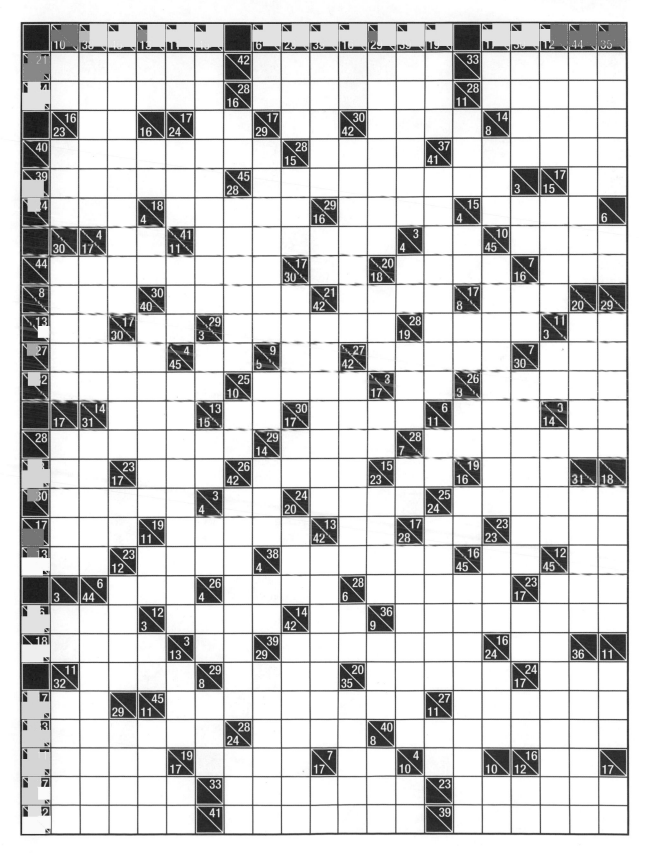

ANSWER, PAGE 93

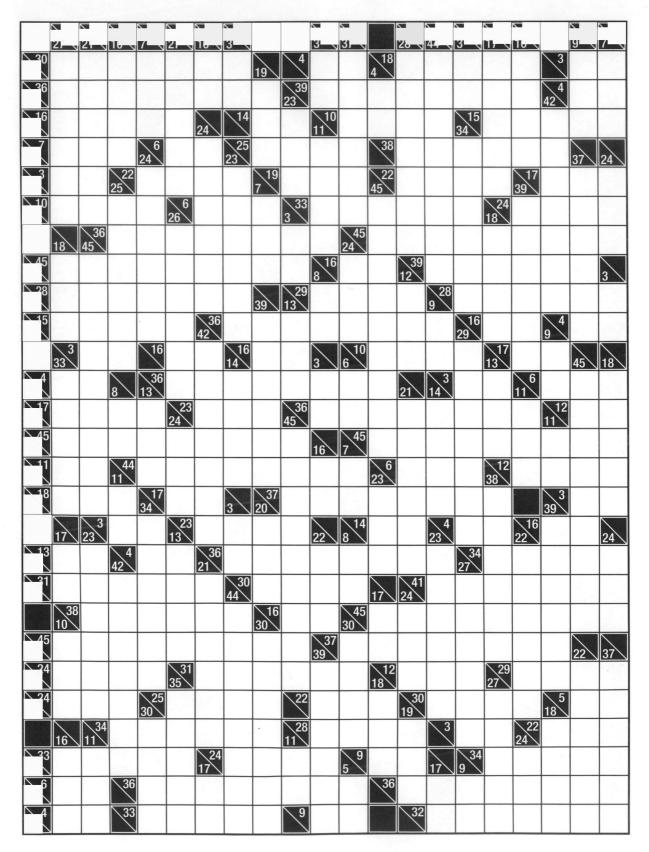

ANSWER, PAGE 93

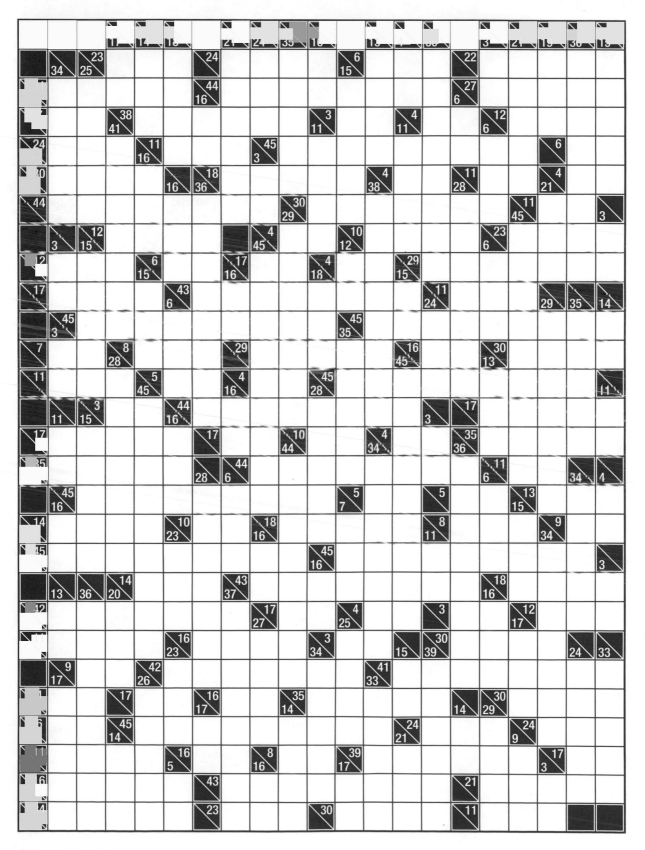

ANSWER, PAGE 94

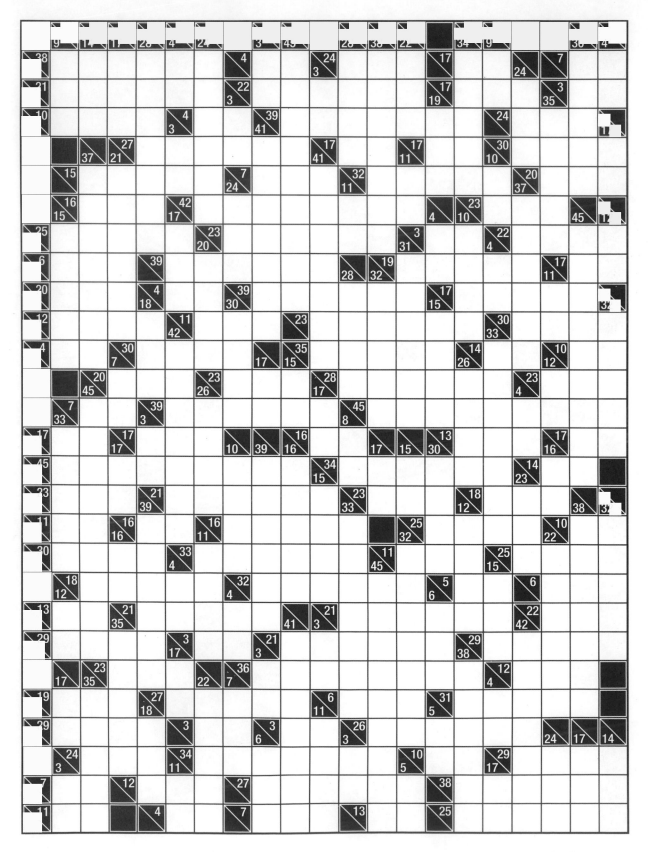

ANSWER, PAGE 94

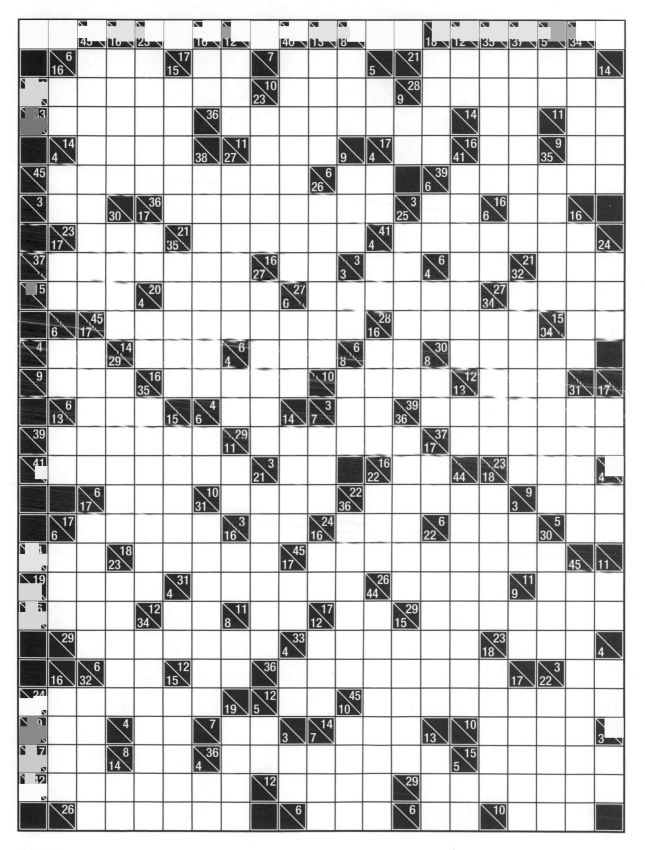

ANSWER, PAGE 94

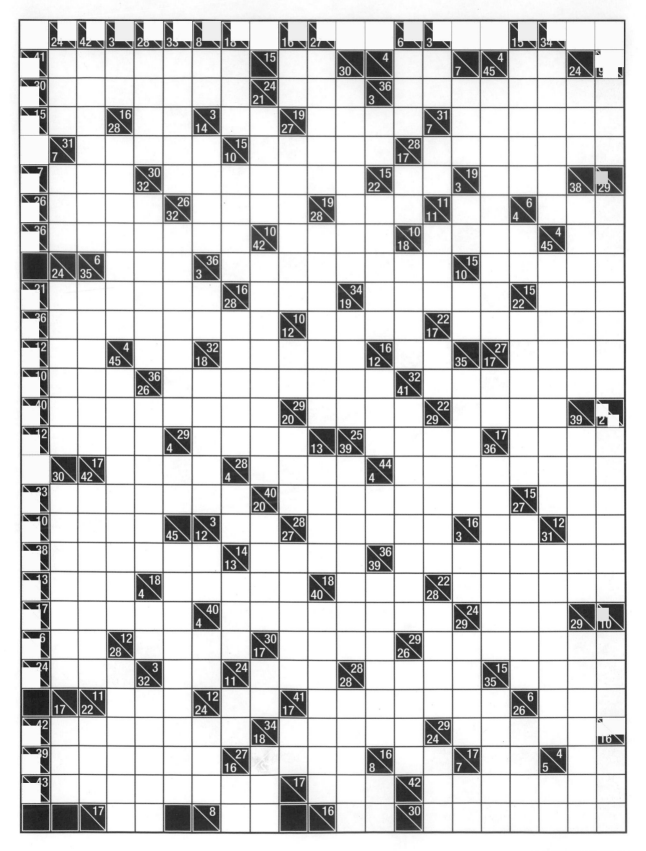

ANSWER, PAGE 94

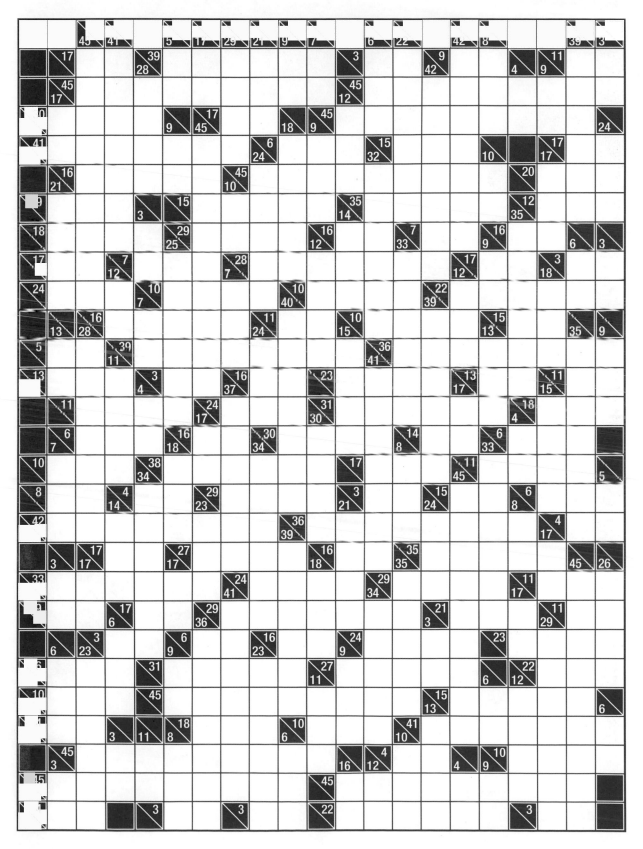

ANSWER, PAGE 95

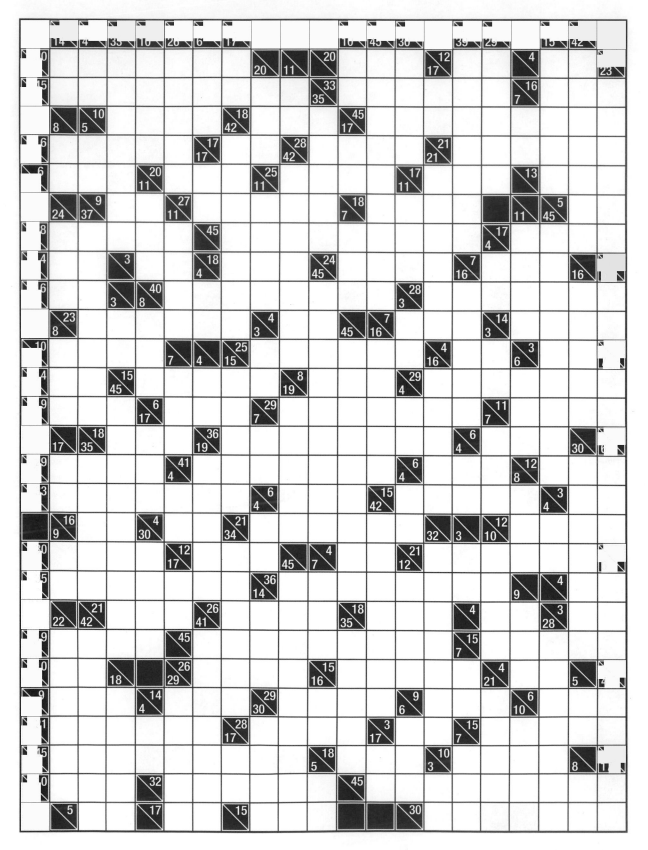

ANSWER, PAGE 95

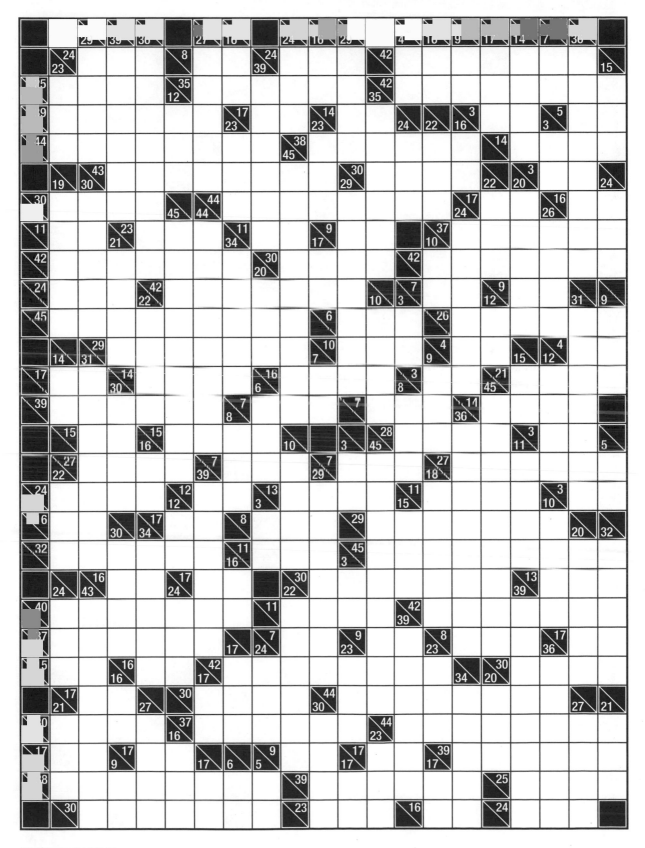

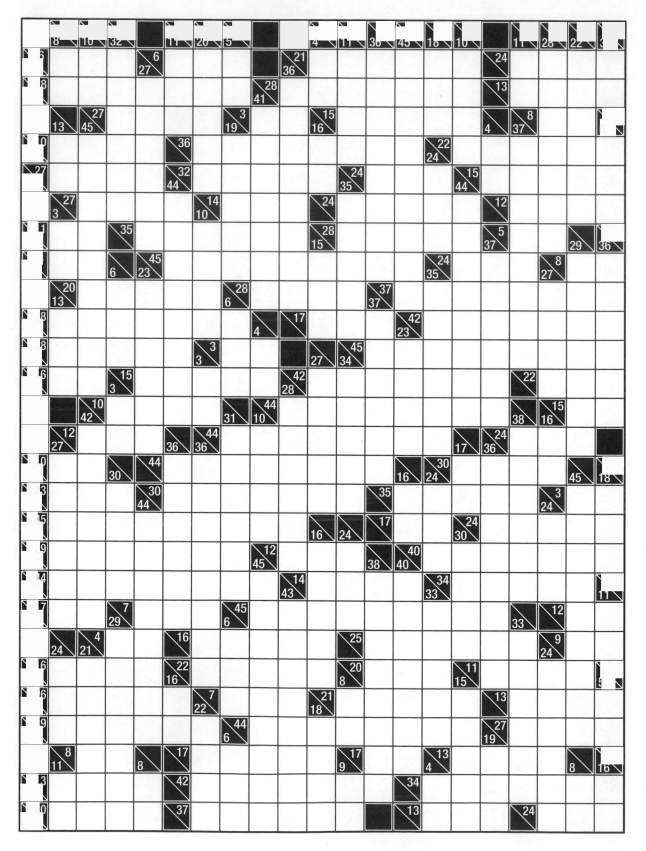

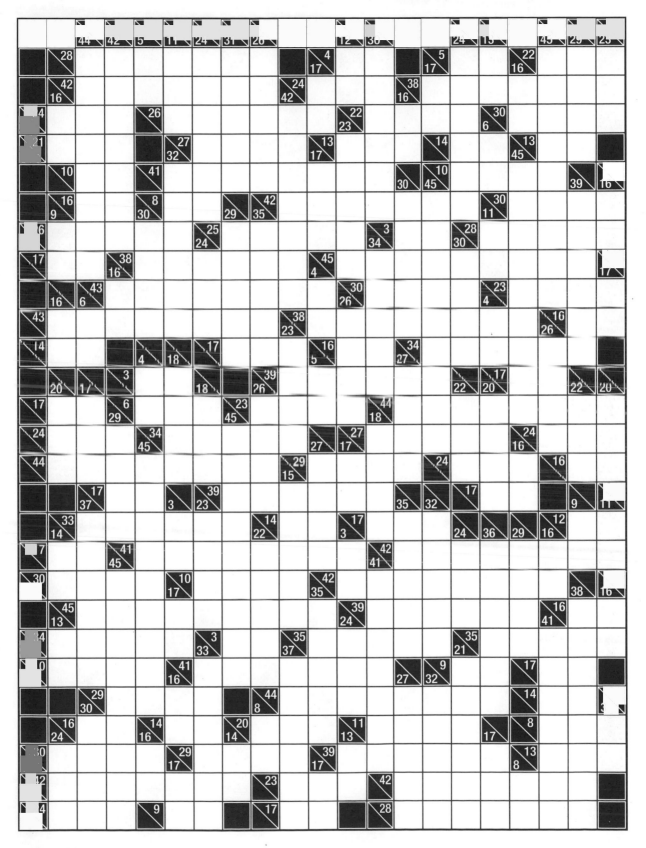

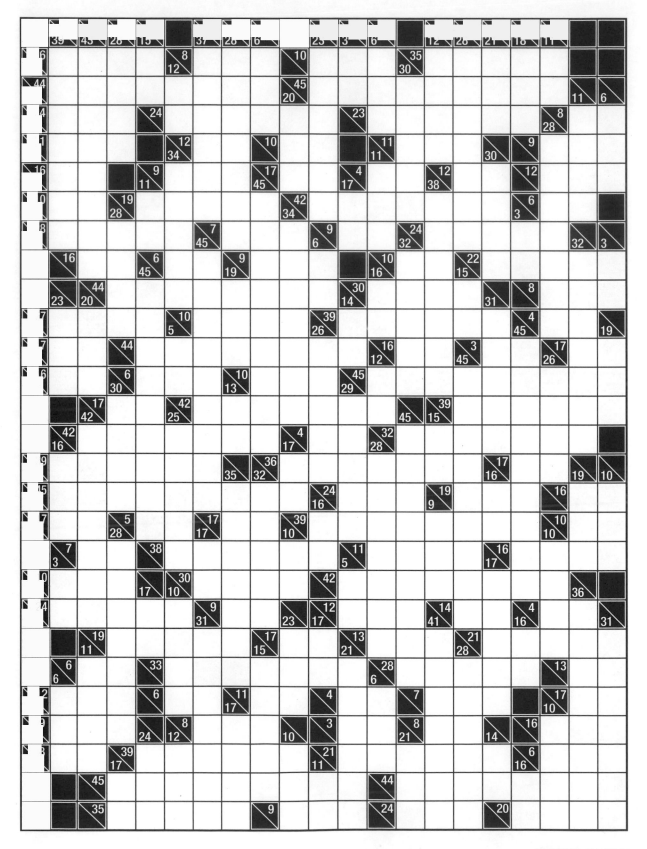

ANSWER, PAGE 96

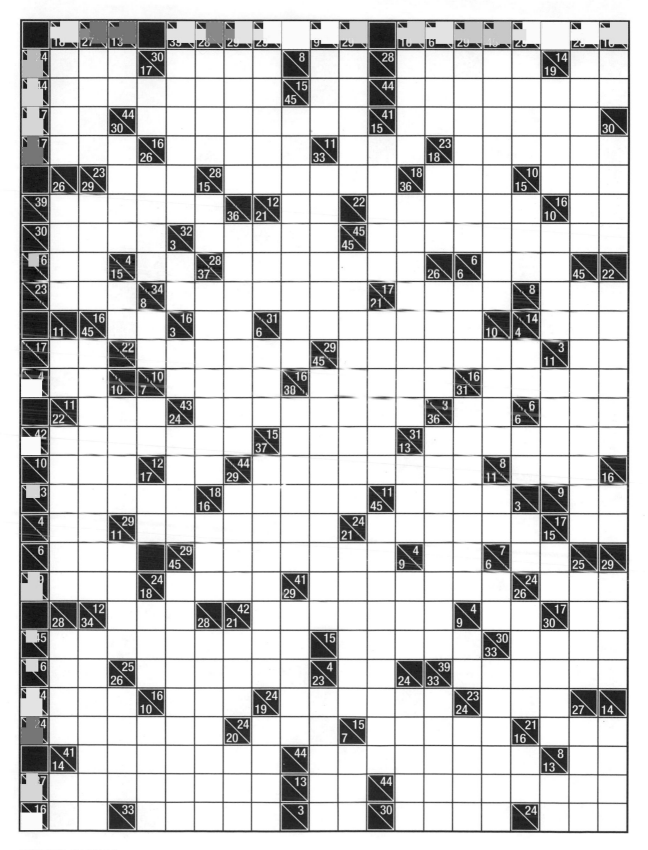

ANSWER, PAGE 96

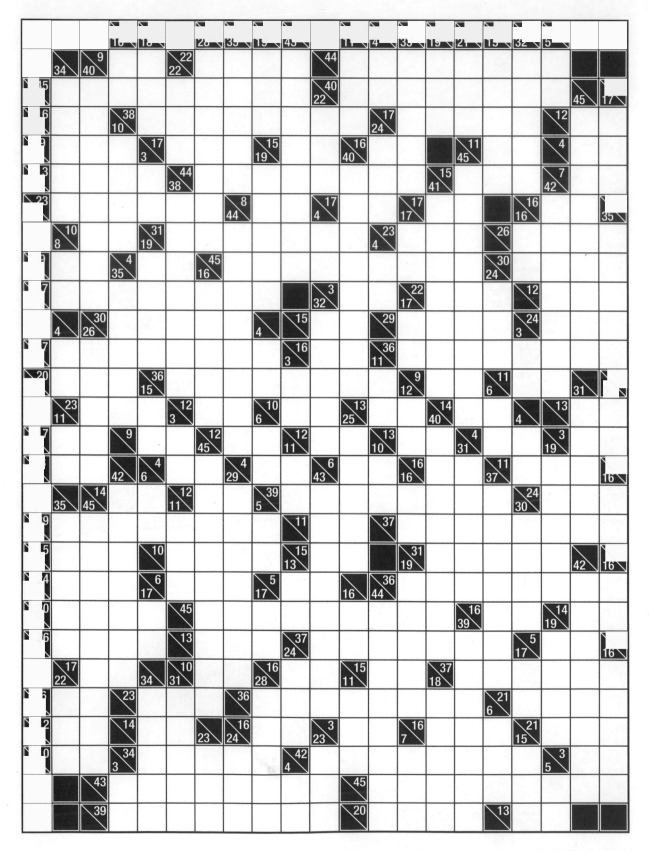

ANSWER, PAGE 96

page 7

page 8

page 9

page 10

page 11

page 12

page 13

page 14

80

page 15

page 16

page 17

page 18

page 19

page 20

page 21

page 22

page 23

page 24

page 25

page 26

page 27

page 28

page 29

page 30

page 31

page 32

page 33

page 34

85

page 35

page 36

page 37

page 38

page 39

page 40

page 41

page 42

page 43

page 44

page 45

page 46

page 47

page 48

page 49

page 50

page 51

page 52

page 53

page 54

page 55

page 56

page 57

page 58

page 59

page 60

page 61

page 62

page 65

page 66

page 67

page 68

page 69

page 70

94

page 71

page 72

page 73

page 74

page 75

page 76

page 77

page 78

96